£7.99

LEARNING RESOURCE CENTRE
THOMAS ROTHERHAM COLLEGE
MOORGATE ROAD
ROTHERHAM
S60 2BE
TEL: 01709 300696

LEARNING RESOURCE CENTRE

TRC
THOMAS ROTHERHAM COLLEGE
A tradition of achievement · A future of opportunity

2 0 DEC 2002		
2 4 FEB 2004		
– 4 MAR 2010		

WITHDRAWN FROM
Thomas Rotherham
College
Learning Resources

D1349458

Thomas Rotherham College

029405

796.8 LEW
(3wl)

THE MARTIAL ARTS

THE
MARTIAL ARTS

PETER LEWIS

Eagle Editions

ACKNOWLEDGMENTS

The author would like to thank Pat Cronshaw of Oriental World, Manchester, England and Maureen Rochford for her time, effort, and patience. Martial Arts Media, England.

The author would like to thank the following for their hard work and cooperation in demonstrating the techniques of their respective martial arts: David Lea, Christopher Thompson, and their students; David Oliver and the students of TAGB; Peter King and Keith LiBahan of the Bujinkan Dojo. Martial arts equipment kindly provided by Meijin Martial Arts, Shepherd's Bush, London.

EDITOR'S NOTE

It is vital that any practitioner of a martial art approach the activity in a disciplined and intelligent fashion. The producers and author of this book therefore stress that tuition from a qualified instructor is essential. Neither children nor adults should attempt to emulate the exercises or techniques illustrated in this book without prior guidance and supervision.

A QUANTUM BOOK

Published by Eagle Editions Ltd
11 Heathfield
Royston
Hertfordshire SG8 5BW

Copyright ©MCMLXXXVII
Quintet Publishing Ltd.

This edition printed 2001

All rights reserved.
This book is protected by copyright. No part of it may be reproduced, stored in a retrieval system, or transmitted in any form or by any means, without the prior permission in writing of the Publisher, nor be otherwise circulated in any form of binding or cover other than that in which it is published and without a similar condition including this condition being imposed on the subsequent publisher.

ISBN 1-86160-430-0

QUMMAR

This book is produced by
Quantum Publishing Ltd
6 Blundell Street
London N7 9BH

Printed in Singapore by
Star Standard Industries Pte Ltd

CONTENTS

A wing chun kung fu sifu strikes a classic pose with the eight cutting broadswords, known popularly as 'Butterfly knives'. Apart from the long pole, the butterfly knives are the only weapons in the system.

INTRODUCTION

On the slopes of the Songshan mountains, in the northern Chinese province of Honan, lies the legendary Shaolin temple, where the sect of Buddhism known as Zen in Japan and Cha'n in China began. It is the purported birthplace of kung fu, or Chinese boxing. Yet although it may be true that many types and styles of kung fu began here, it cannot be realistically argued that all the varieties of kung fu that were and are still practised in China have their roots in Shaolin. Certain schools of thought hold, for instance, that the ancient Greek art of 'pankration', brought to China by the invading armies of Alexander the Great, along with the martial art of Graeco-Roman wrestling, gave birth to some forms of kung fu. And a famous, ancient legend of kung fu relates that a Buddhist monk named Bodhidharma, crossed the Himalayas on foot to arrive at a half-ruined monastery whose monks were in a terrible state of health; Bodhidharma, through a series of health-giving exercises based upon some Indian systems of yoga brought the monks from their emaciated state to a condition of youthful vitality. These exercises, known as the 18 hands of Lo-Han, are popularly believed to be the forerunners of Shaolin temple boxing.

Over a period of time kung fu evolved into five major styles, each taking its name from its creator — Hung, Choy, Mok or Monk, Lau and Li. They are known as the five ancestors, and it is hinted that they were the original founders of the present-day Triad secret societies. The five ancestors are generally regarded as the sole survivors of the Shaolin temple after it was sacked and burned down by the Ching emperor's army. They fled across the Yellow River and went into hiding. After they died, many kung fu systems were developed by their students, and over the next few hundred years more branches of these styles, barely recognizable from the original forms, came into being. Because China is a vast country with many dialects, certain kung fu schools practise styles that are the same but have different names. The 'praying mantis' style for instance, is known in Cantonese as 'tong long' or 'won long'.

The kung fu styles developed at the Shaolin temple were based on the movements of animals. There were five in all, the tiger, crane, leopard, snake and dragon. In later years one or two animals were adopted, along with their natural movements, to form the nucleus for a complete system of kung fu. The southern Chinese style of hung gar ('Hung family') was adapted from the 'Shaolin tiger' system, which also incorporates movements from the 'white crane' style.

Without doubt one of the most popular styles of kung fu today is that of 'wing chun' meaning 'beautiful springtime'. It differs from other kung fu styles in two ways. First, it is the only style that was invented by a woman; and second, it requires only the minimum exertion of force to do the maximum amount of work. The system was originated by a Shaolin nun named Ng Mui, who was an instructor of a kung fu style called 'mui fa chuan', or 'plum flower fist'. In the village where Ng Mui eventually settled, she met a young girl named Yim Wing Chun, to whom she taught her system. Being of slight build, Yim Wing Chun thought that the plum flower fist was too complex, and placed too much reliance on power techniques and strong horse stances more befitting a man than a woman. She needed something less complicated yet totally efficient. Not finding anything among the existing styles to which she was exposed, she created her own, dedicating it to the Buddhist nun who had taught her, but naming it after herself.

The modern-day exponent of the style was the late grandmaster, Yip Man, who was born in the Chinese mainland town of Fatshan, but who left when the Communist takeover was imminent to settle in Hong Kong. One of the most famous students of wing chun was Bruce Lee. It has been suggested that he used wing chun as the basis of his own system of 'jeet kune do' ('way of the intercepting fist').

Two-thirds of wing chun's active principle is based upon hand manoeuvres and subtle, shifting footwork. Contrary to what is often seen in films, very few kicks are employed. The few that are employed are aimed below the waist. The art of wing chun is based on economy of motion. A student of the art learns to defend his centre line (an imaginary line running through the centre of the body, where all the vital organs are housed). The hand techniques make use of the opponent's force to strengthen the practitioner's counter-attack.

Kung fu was primarily developed as a method of self-defence and as an exercise to promote good health. Training in one of the many kung fu styles that exist today consists of the systematic learning and practice of pre-arranged sets known as forms. The simplicity of wing chun is evident from the number of forms, or sets, the student has to master. There are only three — 'sil lum tao', 'chum kui' and 'bil jee'. An interesting sensitivity exercise, developed for students of wing chun, is called 'chi sao', commonly known as 'sticking hands'. This exercise heightens the sensitivity in a student's hands and arms to the point where he can anticipate his opponent's intentions purely by feel.

It has been estimated that many thousands of kung fu styles exist in Asia today. The following list is merely the tip of the iceberg. But it may serve to illustrate how the styles of kung fu that are practised today began.

■ **TAI CHI CHUAN** This is an internal style of kung fu founded by the Taoist mystic, Chang San-Feng (1279–

A tai chi chuan practitioner goes through his routine beside the calm and serenity of a lake, practising the steps of the short form of the exercise.

In the tai chi form, the various movements have distinct names: this tai chi adept performs the 'brush knee hip twist'.

1368). Legend relates that while he was living in the mountains he brewed a hypnotic drink, and after drinking it fell into a deep sleep and dreamed strange dreams. The dreams contained a series of fighting manoeuvres, all of them based on a complete yielding to attack. Upon awakening two days later, he put into practice everything that he had dreamt. The practice consisted of a slow-motion exercise that never stopped. Each movement slipped into the next in an ever-continuing circle. Within two years Chang began to look youthful and was full of vitality. This he attributed to the solo exercise. Some years later he took a disciple named Chen Chia Kou and taught him everything he knew. Later Chen taught the exercise to his own family. The Chen family kept the secret of the form for more than 400 years. A descendant elaborated the exercise and the style eventually split into two branches. The other branch became the yang style that is popular in the West today.

■ **PA-KUA** This is another internal system of kung fu, and means 'eight trigrams', which are the fundamental symbols of the *I-Ching* or *Book of Changes*. The style is based on the premise that if you can defend yourself at the eight compass points covered by the trigrams you will be fully protected from attack. The art has many open-palm strikes and the footwork is based on the circle. There is one central pattern, called the 'da mu hsing' or 'great mother' form, which is the foundation of pa-kua. Emphasis is placed upon developing chi energy (intrinsic power developed by the individual). At advanced stages of learning the student mounts his attacks in twisting, spiralling movements. The twist is done from the waist and generates tremendous power. Pa-kua was brought to light a little more than 400 years ago by its alleged founder, Tung Hai Chuan. But martial arts historians tend to believe that it has its origins almost 5,000 years ago.

■ **HSING-I** This is the last of the three internal styles, invented by a general named Yueh Fei in the 12th century. It is sometimes known as Chinese mind boxing. Although the movements are very graceful, the art stresses the yin-yang principle of complementary opposites, hard and soft. The basic movements are derived from the five Chinese elements of metal, water, wood, fire and earth, each of which has the power to overcome the other. Fire is overcome by water, which in its turn is overcome by earth, earth by wood, wood by metal and metal by fire. In hsing-i these elements are represented by five basic movements: splitting, crushing, pounding, drilling and crossing. Within this framework are the primary movements to cover every angle and direction of attack and defence. The main aim of the practitioner is to

Weapons in the Chinese martial arts number in their thousands; this particular spear-like instrument, called a Kwan-do, (the knife of General Kwan), is one of the better known.

A kung fu instructor assumes a guard attack position with the Chinese sabre. Ancient weapons are still very much a part of the martial arts, although they are now outdated given the range of military hardware now available.

unite his mind with his body. The variations on the basic motions number in their thousands and they are all executed at a very high speed.

■ **PRAYING MANTIS** Also known as 'tong long', this style was invented by a Chinese boxer named Wong Long. After being constantly beaten by fighters from other styles, he retired to practise meditation. One day, sitting in a temple garden, he noticed a grasshopper and a praying mantis locked in battle and he observed that the mantis was fighting in a definite pattern. Facing a much larger and heavier opponent, the mantis would make lightning strikes from its claw-like front limbs, then beat a hasty retreat out of harm's way when the grasshopper retaliated. Fascinated by this display, Wong Long captured the mantis and took it home with him. There he examined the insect's every move by prodding it with a twig. He then formulated a system of fighting derived from the mantis' movements and went back to do battle with the fighters from other systems. So successful was he that he named the new style after the insect.

A variation on this theme is 'seven stars mantis', which is based on the Chinese theory of the heavenly constellations.

■ **BOK HOK PAI** This style is popularly known as the 'white crane'. It was invented by the Tibetan lamas and was originally reserved for the use of the elite corps of bodyguards that protected the emperor of China. It came into being after a lama saw a fight between a white crane and an ape. The lama noticed that as the ape rushed into the attack, the crane would defend by evading and then retaliate with its wings. The lama put together eight techniques from the crane's natural movements and incorporated them with the ape's footwork and grabbing manoeuvres. In bok hok pai, certain elements of the internal systems are involved. 'White crane' techniques exist in many other styles of kung fu.

■ **HUNG GAR** This is an adaptation of the 'Shaolin tiger' system, but it also has aspects of 'white crane' in it. It is characterized by low, wide stances that produce strong solid legs. This low stance is called the horse stance, or ma pu. Hung gar is a strong, hard kung fu style, containing a powerful thrust punch which adepts maintain always results in a knock-out. Hung was taught the style by a Shaolin monk named Gee Seen. The art stresses close-quarter fighting methods.

■ **CHOY LEE FUT** Last, but certainly not least, is this style, originated by Chan Heung. The style began as a secret combat training method for forming the Chinese

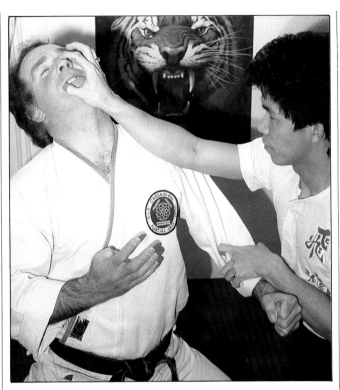

The tiger claw strike can be seen in several kung fu systems. The areas struck with this devastating movement are varied, but the most effective strikes are aimed at the fleshy, sensitive points on the body.

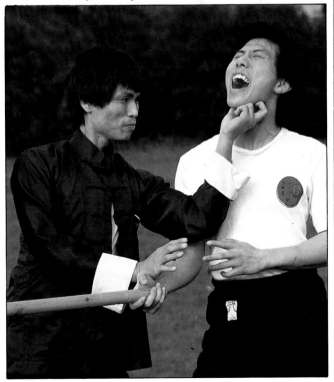

The defender avoids a stick attack and strikes the attacker with a claw grip to the throat.

rebels into a fighting force during the Opium wars of the 19th century. The power source in this style is the waist. Both high and low kicks are involved in the execution of its techniques. This long-range system of boxing involves many deceptive and elusive foot manoeuvres. The hand techniques incorporate hooks and uppercuts, back-fists and roundhouse punches, all delivered with devastating force.

■ **Karate** which means 'empty hand', began on the Japanese island of Okinawa and was greatly influenced by Chinese combat methods and systems. Three main schools of fighting came into being: 'naha-te', 'tomari-te' and 'shuri-te', named after the towns on Okinawa that nurtured them. Okinawan-te, as karate was first known, was introduced into Japan by a mild-mannered Okinawan schoolmaster named Gichin Funakoshi, an expert in the punching and kicking arts of his island homeland, where his teacher was a great master named Azato. Funakoshi put on a display of the art for the emperor of Japan, who was so impressed that he asked him to stay in Japan and teach.

Very soon the school teacher became the idol of Japanese martial arts circles. He opened his first school, or 'dojo' ('training place'), in Tokyo. It was known as 'shotokan', or Shoto's club ('kan' means 'club'), because Funakoshi had previously used the name Shoto as a pen name when he wrote poetry. The name means 'waving pines'. At that time the art was still known as Okinawan-te. But this was later changed into Japanese calligraphy to read karate-do ('way of the empty hand').

In the years that followed Funakoshi's arrival in Japan several other styles were introduced into the country by other Okinawan masters. By the 1930s most leading Japanese universities had thriving karate clubs. Funakoshi's son, Yoshitaka, became something of a driving force behind his father's club, and it is to him that the famous 'mawashi geri', or roundhouse kick, is accredited. Yoshitaka introduced new elements to the art, until gradually the art lost some of its distinctive Okinawan features. Within quite a short time great rivalries grew up between students of different styles. Practitioners of the art broke away to form new styles more attuned to their own ways of thinking, and karate began to fragment.

After World War II karate, which had been banned by the forces of occupation, began to grow once again. In 1955 the Japanese Karate Association (JKA) was formed. Two years later, in April, 1957, Gichin Funakoshi, whom many have termed 'the father of karate' died at the age of 88. But karate was already emerging on the European scene, thanks to the efforts of the French martial arts teacher, Henri Plee. Karate came to England via the work and expertise of an unsung innovator named

The power one can generate in karate is best exemplified by the way adepts smash their limbs through concrete, wood and various other materials. These power breaking techniques are termed tamashiwara.

The three-tined sai is a karate weapon that has its origins on the island of Okinawa. This short, steel, truncheon-like weapon was capable of meeting a full-blown attack from a sword-wielding samurai.

Here a karate teacher thwarts a bo staff attack, using a crossing action with the sai. The trapping action of the sai was very effective in disarming many adversaries.

A spectacular exhibition of a karate tamashiwara breaking technique.

Vernon Bell, who can truly be called the father of English karate.

Modern karate is based upon strikes using punches and kicks combined with many different foot manoeuvres and hip gyrations. Traditionalists, especially from the Okinawan schools, will not take part in modern karate tournaments and competitions, believing that karate was developed for self-defence, not sport. It is generally accepted that the style with the most followers worldwide is Shotokan. At world level, two organizations exist for the governing of karate, WUKO, the World Union of Karate Organizations, and FAJKO, the Federation of All-Japan Karate Organizations. Although karate developed in Japan, that country has never won a team world championship, whereas Great Britain has won it on no less than four occasions — a record unmatched in the history of karate.

Like kung fu, karate is broken up into many styles, each professing to have within its range of techniques the answer to many combat situations. Karate differs from kung fu, however, in that the movements and applications of the various styles are not very distinct from one another. Many diverse schools still come from Okinawa, but it is generally accepted that the mainstay of much of the karate that is practised in the world today is the original shotokan style, brought from Okinawa to Japan by karate's modern-day founder and innovator, Gichin Funakoshi.

The shotokan style of karate arrived in Japan in kata form only. Funakoshi regarded kata as the ultimate expression of his art. The style uses considerable muscle power in the delivery of its movements, which are linear in their application. The style is characterized by long, deep stances.

As Funakoshi's students became adept at the techniques, many broke away from the original shotokan school and formulated systems of their own. The following list provides a brief survey of some of the schools that have become major styles in their own right.

■ **SHOTOKAI** Shotokai karate is similar to shotokan in that the stances are low. Followers of the shotokai style broke away from the parent group of shotokan because they believed that it was deviating from the traditional teachings laid down by Funakoshi. The split was led by many of the older instructors, especially the master, Egami, who disliked the growing tendency to promote karate as a sport.

■ **SHITO-RYU** Hot on the heels of Funakoshi from Okinawa came Kenwa Mabuni, who had studied under the same master, but who also had two other teachers, named Itosu and Higaonna. It was after these two

Two teachers using a system called Hwarang-do applying a combined neck strangulation and head twisting technique. Korea has other martial disciplines quite apart from that of taekwondo.

A Chinese master takes the full force of a spear against the throat. To the left of the picture, two students are pushing the spear: yet amazingly, the sharp point does not penetrate his throat, because his chi gung training will not

teachers that Mabuni named his style. 'Shito' comes from the Japanese characters used to write his teachers' names. Mabuni loved kata, and as a result there are more than 60 in the style. Probably the most characteristic feature of Shito is the avoidance of unnecessary movements which waste time and energy.

■ **SHUKOKAI** One of Mabuni's senior students, Chojiro Tani, split from the organization to develop his own theories on karate for competition, which at the time was gaining great momentum. Tani named this new style, 'shukokai', which means 'way for all'. Through constant research Tani developed faster kicks and higher stances. The higher stances afforded practitioners greater mobility and speedier delivery of techniques. Tani also developed foam-punching pads as training aids. Because the style teaches relaxation before the impact of a punch, it increases acceleration, thus creating a greater force. The basic stance is derived from a person walking and places emphasis upon naturalness.

■ **SANKUKAI** Some years after Tani established his style, history repeated itself and his senior student, Yoshinao Nanbu, left him to found his own school, developed from shukokai, called 'sankukai'. Nanbu gained a certain amount of success on the Japanese karate tournament scene, winning the All-Japan Students Championships three times. For no reason that is known, he then dropped out of the shukokai world, apparently disillusioned. The methods of sankukai bear a marked resemblance to some Chinese kung fu schools.

After establishing sankukai schools in many parts of the world, most notably France, Nanbu left his own organization once again in search of something different. He came up with a system that he has named after himself, 'nanbudo' ('way of Nanbu'). This style is far removed from the Japanese systems he once practised. The leanings are towards the Chinese martial arts and Nanbudo places great stress on a training exercise, called Nanbu Taiso, that has a pronounced Chinese flavour, with its soft, fluid movements.

allow it do so. Chi is an internal, intrinsic energy that, when correctly utilized, can render parts of the adept's body impervious to all outside influences.

■ **WADO-RYU** This style of karate, whose name means 'the way of peace', was founded by Hidenori Otsuka, a senior student of Funakoshi. He spent much of his youth studying jiu jitsu, from which he drew heavily in the formulation of wado-ryu. The style is thought by many to be the fastest of all karate schools. Wado employs very light and fast techniques, preferring evasion to meeting brute force head on. Otsuka was awarded his tenth dan by the brother of the emperor of Japan, and until his death in 1982, just four months short of his 90th birthday, he was the world's oldest practising karateka.

■ **KYOKUSHINKAI** This style of karate, which means 'the way of ultimate truth', was created by Masatatsu Oyama, who was once a student of Shotokan under Gichin Funakoshi. Oyama was Korean by birth and was exposed to both Chinese and Korean martial arts in his youth. He abandoned Shotokan because he was unimpressed by the combat side of the art. He went into self-imposed exile in the mountains of Japan for nearly two years and during this period of isolation formulated a new karate system based on actual combat effectiveness.

Oyama is famous for fighting bulls with his bare hands. In his time he has fought more than 50 of them, killing three outright with a combination of striking techniques. In the early 1970s he introduced a type of tournament competition called knockdown, which, since it allows full power strikes to the body, he believed was the only true test of a karateka's fighting ability. The bout ends when a fighter is knocked to the ground.

■ **GOJU-RYU** This style, whose name means 'hard-soft' style, was developed by an Okinawan named Chojun Miyagi from the original Okinawan style of naha-te. Miyagi's instructor was the great Kanryo Higaonna, who spent much of his youth on mainland China and is known to have studied Chinese boxing methods. After Funakoshi left Okinawa for Japan, Miyago followed. His intention was to open a karate school, but bouts of severe home sickness led him to return to Okinawa. Miyagi devoted all his life to the furtherance of goju. The style remained pure and followed the traditional patterns which he formulated.

■ **GOJU-KAI** A one-time student of goju, Gogen Yamaguchi, broke away from goju-ryu to form his own style of goju-kai. Because Miyagi did not stay in Japan for long periods, it was Yamaguchi who made a great headway with his own system of goju-kai. During World War II Yamaguchi was captured by the Russians and shipped off to a labour camp. Despite terrible deprivation, he managed to survive and returned to Japan after the war. Yamaguchi is known in world karate circles as 'the Cat', because of his remarkable agility. A great deal of emphasis in goju is placed upon special breathing techniques. In the original style no high kicks existed, but with the advent of karate as a sport, some are now used.

As we can see, a wide variety of karate styles has developed from the art's origins. Splinter groups follow splinter groups in quick succession. Karate has made great strides in the fields of sport and entertainment in recent years, so that there are now semi- and full-contact karate sports as well as kickboxing. Some people see this as the natural progression for the martial art to take; purists and traditionalists look upon the changes with disdain. But of one thing we can be certain: karate has something for everyone.

■ **TAEKWONDO** The name taekwondo literally translated means 'way of the foot and fist'. Although taekwondo is basically a modern development, its roots can be traced back nearly 1500 years, to the indigenous native style of 'tae-kyon'. A Buddhist monk named Wong

Kwang is said to have originated the five principles that form the basis of taekwondo.

These five principles were: be loyal to your king; be obedient to your parents; be honourable to your friends; never retreat in battle; kill with justice.

The Korean peninsula consisted of three kingdoms, the smallest of which was called Silla. Because Silla was always under attack from its powerful and war-like neighbours, the nobility formed an elite corps of fighting men to defend them. This group was called the 'Hwarang-do', which means Way of the Flowering Manhood. Their combat methods incorporated the fighting arts of tae-kyon and soo-bak. Eventually, Silla managed to unite the three kingdoms under one banner. Towards the end of the 10th century, through internal political strife, Silla was overthrown and the kingdom of Koryo was founded. It became compulsory for all young men to learn martial arts. For over 500 years compulsory training in tae-kyon and soo-bak existed. There then followed a decline, and the old arts would have been lost, had it not been for the Buddhist monks who kept the arts alive in their mountain refuges. By the time of the Japanese occupation in 1909, the art was virtually dead. The Japanese invaders added to this a ban on the practice of all martial arts, in an attempt to suppress the Korean nationalist spirit. Japanese influence remained strong in Korea until 1945, so it was only natural that some of the Japanese martial arts would filter through. The next influence on the development of taekwondo came from General Choi Hong Hi. He had learned the old art of tae-kyon from his master, Han Il Dong. The general then went on to learn Shotokan karate and gained a black belt in the art. After the Second World War, Choi Hong Hi joined the new Korean army and taught his martial skills to the men under his command. In 1954 Choi became head of the board concerned with the development of a unified martial system. It was at his suggestion that the name taekwondo be used, because it bore a close similarity to the old name of tae-kyon. At a special conference of martial experts on 11 April 1955, taekwondo became the national martial art of Korea. The first competitive championships were held in the following year. In 1966 the first international taekwondo federation was formed. Owing to unexplained political pressures, General Choi then left the country. His organization, the ITF (International Taekwondo Federation), went with him. The Korean government quickly set up a rival organization to the ITF, called the World Taekwondo Federation (WTF). Today both these groups exist although the WTF is by far the larger of the two.

Apart from China, it is to Japan that we must look for the largest influence on the martial arts. One of the first

Japanese arts to be recognised in the West was jiu jitsu, 'the art of flexibility'. It was jiu jitsu, with its vast range of locks, holds, and strangulation techniques, that the armed forces of many countries made the foundation for their unarmed combat training.

Jiu jitsu's sporting form, that of judo, 'the gentle way' was looked at as a method for training law enforcement officers in arrest and hold techniques. Judo, the brain-

Jiu jitsu is a Japanese grappling art that incorporates a myriad of locks, throws and breaking techniques. An attacker can be quite literally tied up in an excruciatingly painful arm twist in seconds.

These tonfa were originally the handles of a manually operated rice grinder. They were adapted to protect the forearms against strikes from various weapons.

child of Jigoro Kano (1860–1938) is a less lethal form of jiu jitsu. Kano regarded his judo as more of a sport than a fighting system. In 1964, judo became an Olympic sport, and remains the only martial art in the games. Because of the limited techniques that judo offered, some police forces eventually opted for aikido. Aikido ('the way of harmony') was created by Morihei Uyeshiba, and is based on avoiding conflict by neutralizing an opponent's attacks. The art is characterized by flowing, circular movements, and the use of ki, a vital energy that is cultivated in all its adherents. Uyeshiba developed the techniques of aikido from his study of the many styles of jiu jitsu in Japan. It is often said that the aikido adept resembles the eye of a hurricane. He remains quiet within himself, but he is difficult to overcome, because of the circular energy that surrounds him.

Specialization in weaponry has attracted a large following in the West. The most popular is kendo ('the way of the sword'). Kendo is a system of sporting combat in which the participants try to score points by striking the opponent with a bamboo, imitation sword, called a shinai. The uniform consists of a long split skirt called a hakama, a special armoured breastplate, a full head mask, and thickly padded gloves. Kendo originated from an early battlefield art called kenjutsu, which is the ancient samurai art of the sword. Kenjutsu was not a sport: it was simply the art of killing an enemy as quickly as possible.

The further one explores the vast realm of martial disciplines, the more strange and exotic weapons and arts one finds. The Japanese art of staff fighting for example, is termed Bojutsu, and vaguely resembles old English quarterstaff fighting. Participants fight with poles measuring around six feet in length. Another weapon still used is that of the Naginata. This is very much a woman's weapon. It resembles a European halberd. Today, women in Japan have formed naginata leagues. The once razor sharp blades have been replaced by wooden ones tipped with rubber.

Indigenous martial disciplines have existed even in western cultures. Britain had various forms of wrestling, such as Cumberland, Westmorland, and catch-as-catch-can. The nearest any western fighting technique has come to the eastern martial arts, is in the French art of 'la Savate'. It is thought that the style originated somewhere in the far East, and was introduced in to France by sailors. La Savate began life in the backstreets of Marseilles. It was a method that the footpads (street robbers) used for fighting. It is interesting that the art does not include hand strikes: in a series of elaborate hand-stands, the savate expert can flip his feet in the air and kick to the opponent's head. Various leaping kicks were also included in the range of techniques.

Although China and Japan were the central areas for martial arts development over the last 2,000 years, many other countries in southeast Asia developed indigenous fighting systems, each of which, though perhaps not so well known, has produced great masters and thousand-years old traditions. The Philippines, for instance, devel-

oped the stick art of escrima, or 'arnis de mano' ('harness of the hand'), in which the combatants fight with two hardwood sticks. Their expertise is incredible and on many occasions they defeated Spanish invaders who were armed with swords and lances. Because the Philippines were being constantly invaded, the islanders, known as Moros, retreated to the jungle and waged a continual guerrilla war against the enemy, abandoning their escrima sticks in favour of short, razor-sharp daggers which could be more easily wielded in the jungle's dense foliage.

Escrima is only one branch of a whole art of the Filipino islanders, called kali. Unusually, the martial art of kali teaches the use of weapons first and empty-handed techniques last. At the turn of this century, when the United States occupied the islands, the Moro tribesmen exacted such a deadly toll of American soldiers by their throat-cutting tactics that the commander-in-chief, General 'Blackjack' Pershing, instituted the wearing of

leather thongs around the necks of the American marines. This protection earned the soldiers the nickname of 'leathernecks', which still persists to this day.

After World War II many Filipinos emigrated to the United States and settled in and around Stockton in southern California. There they introduced escrima to eager young American martial artists and the last five years have seen escrima and kali grow from strength to strength.

Media publicity has brought the once secret martial arts very much to the forefront and styles have begun to emerge from many countries in southeast Asia. In Thailand, for example, there is practised an ancient art of war which has developed over the centuries into a highly exciting spectator sport. This is known as muay thai, or Thai boxing. In its early days this hand-and-foot method of combat was extremely dangerous, even when it was developed into a sport. Before the 1930s, when formal rules and regulations were introduced, contestants would

A Thai boxing master executing a flying kick. Note the way he prevents his opponent from retaliating by blocking the intended kick with his own back leg.

get into a ring to fight wearing crude boxing gloves made of hemp. Often these gloves were dipped in a mixture of glue and ground glass to produce terrifying results. Almost one in three fights ended in the death of one of the competitors. Perhaps the most lethal blow in Thai boxing was the elbow strike to the temple, which is now banned.

Towards the mid-1970s Thai boxing was introduced into the United States, where it has become very popular, partly because it resembles another art introduced at that time, called full-contact karate.

Full-contact, as it is generally known, was the brain-child of a few martial artists who were tired of the con-trolled sparring methods allowed in karate and taek-wondo. They decided to don boxing gloves and fight in a square ring, like professional boxers, so that they could employ full-power kicks and punches against one another, instead of having to let their attacks fall just short of a designated target area. Almost overnight this new sport was a huge success. Within two years tele-vision gave it air time and a new spectator sport was born.

A little later on, semi-contact came into existence. This allows competitors to fight under virtually the same rules as their full-contact brothers, but strikes and kicks are judged more on a points system, points being awarded for perfection of technique rather than for pounding a competitor into the ground or knocking him out. Thai boxing has also been introduced into Europe, where it has become very popular, with matches and tourna-ments being held on a regular basis.

Before long another form of combat came to the attention of the world's martial arts population. It was called kickboxing and was a combination of muay thai and full-contact karate in one. Associations were formed and rules instituted, and kickboxing gained a high degree of popularity. Low kicks to the legs are not allowed, but apart from that and a few other rules, kickboxing is simi-lar to the other martial art ring-sports.

Traditionalists from many branches of the martial arts feel that many modern practitioners, drawn to the arts as sport, are missing their true meaning and aiming only for self-gratification and glory. Individuals begin training in a martial art for many different reasons, for fitness, for self-defence or purely for the discipline that it offers. What-ever the reason, once the journey on that path is commenced, the martial artist can travel down many avenues. It is up to him to ascertain how far he wishes to travel and by what route. The purpose of this book is to aid the reader by showing him what is entailed at the beginning stages of four of the most popular and wide-spread martial arts. As it is said in the East, 'only by seeking, can one find'.

A typical example of an eclectic fighting art: a Mugendo professor executes a roundhouse kick against his student. Today's martial artists are constantly looking at other forms of combat technique in order to broaden and improve their own fighting methods.

A semi-contact fighter executes a jumping spinning roundhouse kick. Semi-contact karate is one of the most popular forms of competition fighting. It started in the USA and spread across the world in less than four years.

CHAPTER ONE

KUNG FU

KUNG FU EQUIPMENT

1 A black kung fu suit: the suit is black because, in China, white is the colour of mourning. It is different to the Japanese and Korean suits in that, although it is loose fitting, it has buttons and a high Mandarin collar. 2 The blade of the long sword (wu shu jien) is made of aluminium. It is used in many weapon forms (katas), notably in tai chi chuan. 3 The three-section staff was an ancient battlefield weapon. 4 The wing chun butterfly knives are called baht jam do, which translates roughly as 'eight-cutting broadswords'. The heavy, cleaving blade was devastating with just one blow.

The martial arts are unique. One trains in the arts of war, yet the ultimate goal is peace. One of the vehicles for that inner peace and tranquillity is the Chinese cultural legacy known as kung fu.

Many people, both men and women, take up kung fu, not all of them for the same reasons. Some see it as the perfect exercise for keeping fit; others train purely for self-defence purposes. But whatever it is that they seek, this Chinese martial art will, somewhere along the road of disciplined training, provide it. Because it places little emphasis on sheer physical strength, kung fu is a discipline open to young and old alike.

Beginning a martial art such as kung fu has many pitfalls. Each individual experiences his own problems. For one person it may be the hard training regimens involved in the exercises. For another it may be frustra-tion at the discovery that his body lacks the co-ordination needed to perform a precise movement correctly.

The key to enjoying the martial arts is perseverance. The practitioner has to get beyond his accustomed, Western modes of thinking even to glimpse beneath the surface and understand what kung fu is all about. The most important thing to remember when learning the art of kung fu is to take your time. Take each lesson step by step. Accumulate movements slowly and assimilate them thoroughly. Do not cast aside a movement that one feels is perhaps a little silly or archaic. These arts of war have been nurtured over thousands of years. They have stood the test of time. So, when a movement is taught to you and you cannot understand the meaning behind it, do it as directed, practising it a thousand times if necessary. With repetition comes understanding.

■ The leopard stance.

■ The tiger stance.

BEGINNING KUNG FU TRAINING

The first step to learning the fascinating skills of kung fu is to seek out an instructor. This may be done by thumbing through the pages of the local telephone directory, then calling in to watch the training at the club selected. There are many different styles of kung fu practised in the world today; so a beginner should look around before deciding which of them best suits his particular requirements. When entering a kung fu club for the first time, there are certain principles of etiquette to be observed. The first time one addresses an instructor, one should call him sifu, which means 'father' and is always applied to a Chinese kung fu instructor in accordance with the art's long family traditions. The same title is also used for a woman of the same rank. All kung fu systems are called families, and although good manners and etiquette are deemed essential, they are perhaps not as strict as those of Japanese martial art systems.

A club where kung fu is practised is called a kwoon, which means 'training place', and is known as the kung fu home. New students are informed that Chinese kung fu adopts many different mantles, and is a system for both self-defence and the improvement of one's health and physical well-being. Kung fu incorporates ideas from many disciplines, including wrestling, with its locks, holds, throws and takedowns. Its entire offensive and defensive repertoire is based upon animal fighting concepts. The ancient Chinese observed the fighting methods of certain animals and adapted them to form the basis of a martial arts system. Many of the kung fu systems were based upon just five animals — the tiger,

■ The dragon stance.   ■ The snake stance.   ■ The crane stance.

■ The attention position 1: the correct distribution of body weight is essential.

2 Most of the body weight is supported on the back leg, and the leading arm strikes with the leopard paw to the face.

3 The leading arm then withdraws back to the body in preparation for the next move.

■ The double fist strike 1: aimed at the head and sternum simultaneously.

2 The double fist strike: side view.

3 Upon impact, the whole of the body weight follows through, for maximum effect.

■ The manoeuvrability of the leopard stance: the student can, by use of deft footwork in which all the weight is centred on the back leg, spring forwards, backwards and sideways to defend against attack from any angle.

■ The tiger claw form 1: the initial stance.

2 With the fingertips of the leading hand curled around in readiness for a claw-like strike, the rear arm guards against any counter-attack.

3 The tiger claw attack: front view. Note that the body leans forwards, with most of the weight on the leading leg.

4 The leading arm then pulls back to cover the head against an impending kick from the opponent.

5 From a crouched stance, the student snakes out the lower arm in a tiger claw towards the groin area, to grap and rip.

6 Having completed the movement, the student draws back his leading leg to adopt an attention stance, with his arms already forming a second claw.

7 A second attack is then instituted, using the same technique.

8 The attack completed, the student draws up into an attention stance.

9 The form continues with the student initiating an attack from the opposite direction: most forms in kung fu cover all directions of the compass.

10 the attack continues from a front-facing position.

11 If necessary, the tiger claw can be converted into a full-fist technique in order to deliver the most effective strike.

■ A leading hand tiger claw technique is applied. Note that the rear hand protects the body against a counter strike by an opponent.

■ The crane hooking block 1: a front punch is blocked by the defender who steps to the side.

2 The block is then converted into a grab; the defender pulls the attacker forwards, who is unbalanced, partly by his own momentum.

3 The attacker's body weight drives him head-on into a claw strike that covers the whole area of the face.

crane, dragon, leopard and snake. Each animal style stresses the development of a particular skill: the crane exemplifies balance; the dragon, spirit and agility; the leopard, strength; the tiger, bone; and the snake, internal power and the ability to strike at vital points of the body.

THE BASIC POSITIONS

All training in kung fu begins with the laying down of a solid foundation. Each technique that is learned at the early stages is called a basic position. The principles of basic training are really quite simple; the student learns many various movements which are then strung together to form an effective technique. The hand positions and stances are learned within the first few weeks. The new student will be expected to train daily at his home and attend a club training session at least twice a week. Gradually, over a period of two or three months, he will be taught the basic elements of the art of kung fu.

The first basic stance is called 'ma pu', or the 'horse stance'. This straddle-leg stance is the basic defensive position. The knees are bent as if one were riding a horse, with the feet parallel and about one yard apart. The body weight is distributed evenly on both legs and the back is straight. Because of its low centre of gravity, this stance not only provides excellent balance, but also makes it easy to kick and strike from the side. It is a typical kung fu combat stance. In ancient times Chinese students would stand in this stance for hours upon end until their legs felt like lead. Modern training is much less arduous.

Unlike the Japanese martial art of karate, kung fu employs very few kicks, and those that are used rarely go higher than the waist. The Chinese believe that to stand on one leg while kicking with the other unbalances the practitioner and places him at a disadvantage. Film producers have ignored this fact and have made films in

功
夫

■ Correct body positioning 1: the sifu indicates to the student the importance of body positioning when delivering an attack.

■ Ma pu: (the horse stance).

2 The student, duly corrected, now punches to the sternum, aware that his rear hand must act as a guard against a counter-attack. A counter is instituted and blocked by a downward palm technique.

■ The horse stance: side view. Note the perfectly erect torso.

which masters jump ten feet in the air, thrashing out kicks in all directions. Yet at times kung fu appears to contradict itself, professing one thing while seeming to do the opposite. Thus, although it has been stated that there are practically no high kicks in kung fu, the practitioner who emulates the crane is training his legs for the highest possible kicks. This exercise is done, however, not because the practitioner will use high kicks, but to teach him balance, so that he can execute kicks that are allowed with precision and accuracy.

Learning the basics involves knowledge of the various hand positions. In the West the closed fist is considered

almost the only effective weapon to be used in unarmed combat. The Chinese believe the exact opposite. The Chinese consider the clenched fist as a weak and vulnerable weapon, to be used rarely and only if it is aimed at a soft part of the body. The open hand is much stronger and less prone to injury. Furthermore, its flexibility and power of movement are considerably greater, so that less power is needed to deliver a blow. Because open hands are relaxed, and the muscles not taut, the speed of delivery is increased by almost 50 per cent.

In kung fu the hands take their shape from the particular animals whose fighting techniques the practitioner is

■ A variation on the tiger claw attack.

■ The sifu demonstrates a full head-on tiger claw attack; the ripping and gouging movements make it very hard to defend against.

imitating. If adopting the tiger style, for instance, the hands would be shaped like claws. When attacking in this style, the student would not punch; rather, he would gouge and claw, rip and tear at his opponent. The list of hand movements and positions in kung fu is endless, since every part of the hand is considered to be a defensive weapon. A beginner usually learns first the open-palm strike, the simplest hand-strike in kung fu. The target area for this blow is the face. One slapping movement with the open palm, aimed at an opponent's nose, is enough to deter most adversaries. Another hand technique that is often used is the crane's beak, in which all the fingertips of the hand are joined together to form something that resembles a bird's beak. With a swift in and out action the practitioner strikes at his attacker's eyes.

Each of the various hand movements has a specific job to do, determined by range, angle, position and target. The Chinese believe that the Western habit of nearly always punching to the face is of little use, since there are no vital organs housed there save for the eyes and nose. Kung fu artists aim their attacks at the body's vital spots, which are said to be located along an imaginary line running down the middle of the body. Starting

■ A classical defence and attack stance: the low body position allows the adept either to drop to the floor or leap into the air, depending on the given situation.

■ A dramatic and menacing example of the front tiger claw attack in action.

■ The X block 1: kung fu is well suited to female self-defence. The defender blocks an attempted punch to the face.

2 The X block is then pushed upwards, taking the attacker's fist with it.

3 She breaks her X block defence, once the fist is out of harm's way.

4 With one arm still holding the attacker's fist at bay, the defender draws back her other arm, ready to counter-attack.

5 She then counters with a palm heel strike to the attacker's nose.

■ 1 Application of the fingertip strike 1: the attacker moves in from the side. The defender senses the impending danger.

2 She turns quickly on the balls of her feet to meet the advance. The attack is warded off with a forearm block.

3 The defender counters with a fingertip strike to her attacker's throat.

from the top, a typical kung fu attack would concentrate on the eyes, nose, throat, larynx, sternum, heart, solar plexus and groin. Each point has the power, when struck forcibly, to incapacitate an opponent. The average Westerner fails to take into account the fact that there are so many weak points on the human body. It is therefore advisable that all practice be carried out with extreme caution.

A good kung fu man never stands rigidly; his posture has to appear natural and relaxed. His arms hang loosely, but not limply, by his side, the legs are slightly bent, and the body is turned towards the side. This posture is ideal for facing a confrontation, because the arms are so loose that they can swing into action to block an attack and strike at the same time. The slightly bent legs enable him to spring into action immediately, whereas stiff-locked legs would first have to become unlocked before attacking. Vital seconds, and the advantage of surprise, would thus be lost. Also, if the legs were stiff and locked, a low kick from the attacker might break the leg or the knee-

■ The correct Chinese horse stance, with which all beginners start their kung fu training.

■ A kung fu practitioner can adopt any pose that suits the situation. At times, the stance looks very similar to that of a western boxer, as in this crouched position

■ This free sparring pose adopts a more upright stance.

功
夫

cap. A rigid leg has no alternative but to snap; a bent leg, having give in it, can at least straighten upon the impact of an aggressor's kick. By presenting the body to the side, at an angle, the defender limits his attacker's target area. All his vital organs are safely out of harm's way.

FOOT PATTERNS & MOVEMENTS

Once a student has learned how to hold his hands in defensive and offensive positions (in many cases the positions are identical) and he has become familiar with the basic stances, he progresses to footwork patterns and movements.

Good footwork consists essentially in the ability to move swiftly from one position to another without sacrificing balance. Beginners often make the mistake of looking down when they are moving from one position to another, thus breaking the cardinal first rule of combat, which is never to take your eyes off your opponent. A student has to be versatile enough to evade an attack by

■ This free fighting natural position, with the student leaning forward, allows for maximum manoeuvrability.

■ When faced with a hostile situation, or when sparring, a good kung fu student always presents a side-on target to his adversary. This both presents a smaller target for the opponent to strike at, and helps to protect the vital organs.

■ Close-in forearm training 1: a training method designed to develop sensitivity and fast reaction.

2 The attacker strikes from close range, but not with full power. The attack is blocked and instantly countered; the counter is then blocked by the first attacker, who in turn counters, and so on. This tit for tat procedure helps to develop awareness of angles of attack.

3 After a few minutes, the mind cannot cope with the speed, and one partner usually finishes up tangled in a knot.

■ As an alternative to the fan strike (right), the defender can retaliate by substituting a palm heel strike.

stepping, hopping or jumping to the side, while slipping into another more advantageous position in order to counter-strike. If he looks down at his feet, his opponent will seize the opportunity to attack. As the old saying goes, 'if the first one doesn't get you, the second one will'.

To be able to change from one foot position to another requires coordination and balance, which can be achieved only by practising over and over again. Forfeit speed for perfection. At the beginning speed is not essential; balance is. Speed comes partly from good footwork anyway.

New students are taught foot patterns from the basic horse stance. Adopting this stance, keeping your left foot in place, take a wide step to the side with your right foot. Then slide the left foot into place next to your right foot. Both feet should now be next to each other. Continue moving by once again stepping out with your right foot, then sliding the left foot into place next to it. Practise this the full length of the training hall and then switch feet, keeping the right foot in place and stepping out with the left. This foot changeover has to be repeated hundreds of times before any kind of perfection is achieved. As the

technique becomes easier, the changeover comes to be executed with a kind of skipping motion and short distances are covered at great speed.

Deflective body movements also play an important part in avoiding an attack. The turning stance is probably the easiest method of parrying a blow without strength or effort. Its subtle body shift has the power to nullify a forceful attack from an opponent. It is techniques such as the turning stance that enable kung fu to be practised without the requirement of great physical strength. If a woman in her own defence were to throw a straight punch to the face of a man weighing eighteen stone, the consequences would almost certainly be dire. But if the woman were to employ the kung fu turning stance, the outcome would be quite different. As the attacker rushes forwards to launch a straight punch to the face, the defender stretches out her left arm to counter it. It must be pointed out, however, that the defender's outstretched arm tries, not to block the punch, but merely to guide it away by utilizing the turning stance, thus changing her front stance to a side stance. In this way she guides the attacker's punch right past her with a successful deflec-

3 The splayed fan strikes the attacker's face; the iron spines make contact with the head.

■ Fan defence 1: The attacker strikes with a low punch and is stopped with a strike to the wrist bone.

2 The defender grasps the attacker's fist to prevent a second punch and strikes outwards with the fan now fully open.

■ Application of techniques 1: the attacker and defender assume positions.

2 The attacker is blocked by a rising elbow, a technique from the crane system.

3 Before the attacker can employ a second technique, the defender strikes to the face with the palm.

tion. As the aggressor is propelled forward by his own weight, strength and momentum, he may be struck in the throat by any one of the basic hand techniques. The aggressor's own forward momentum even strengthens the force of the counter-blow against him.

Many of the basic foot patterns in kung fu appear to be simple in their execution and the fact is that they are. Yet it often happens that when a new kung fu student enters a kwoon, with pre-conceived ideas about fighting, and is shown basic techniques that look as though they were aimed at primary school level, he looks for more in those techniques than there actually is. The ancient kung fu masters often told students a parable to illustrate the need to come to kung fu with an uncluttered mind. The story relates that an abbot was pouring tea for a young novice monk who had recently joined the monastery to learn kung fu. When the cup was full, the abbot kept on pouring the tea. After a few seconds the novice, with tea spilling out of the cup and down his arms, cried, 'stop! no more will go in'. The abbot smiled and likened the novice to the overflowing cup of tea: 'To learn, you first have to empty your cup, in order to assimilate something new'.

THE PARRIES AND BLOCKING PRINCIPLES OF KUNG FU

As the first law of kung fu is defend, then attack, the student who has gained knowledge of the basic strikes, has next to be trained in parries and blocking manoeuvres to enable him effectively to stop a punch without being hit himself. At this point in the student's instruction his sifu will watch to see that he brings into play all the previous concepts of footwork, stance, balance and counterstriking. As we have seen, it is far easier to parry a direct

■ The double palm block 1: the attack to the face is blocked immediately.

2 Maintaining his hold on the attacker, the defender uses his block to pull the attacker onto a rising knee to the stomach. The attacker's own momentum pushes him forward onto the blow.

■ A variation on the double palm block 1: this time, the defender initiates a low kick sweep to the back of the attacker's kneecap.

2 The kick is applied, and at the same time, weight is brought to bear on the attacker's trapped arm, pushing him down.

■ Application of leopard techniques 1: the attacker punches.

2 The defender avoids the blow, using the movement of the leopard to shift deftly to the side, while he institutes his own counter-attack of a leopard strike to the face.

3 The defender's strike converts into an elbow slam to the side of the jaw.

4 As the attacker falls backwards after the initial blow, he is floored by another full-force elbow strike across the throat.

blow than to stop it forcibly. All parrying in kung fu is done by a light brushing action, rather than a hard block.

The kung fu practitioner uses his opponent's strength to aid him in this task. Correct parrying requires of the defender only a simple movement of the wrist. This principle of meeting force with softness permeates the whole of the Chinese martial arts. The less energy spent in defending, the more strength remains to attack and defeat the enemy.

Many of the parrying and blocking principles of kung fu involve grabbing and pushing away. All that is needed is to throw an oncoming punch off course. But here again the Western beginner, either through fear or lack of confidence in his own ability, often puts too much into the actual blocking technique and this overworking leads inevitably to failure. It gradually becomes clear to the student that kung fu is more than just a series of physical body movements. The art begins to seep deep into his psychological being.

It is very common for new students to give up after about three months. Some drop out, of course, because kung fu really does not suit them. More often, however, the cause is simple frustration at being unable to adapt to the technical demands of the art. Practising kung fu puts a person in touch with himself or herself; his or her own failings are brought out into the open. People who find it difficult to cope with this self-inflicted mental ridicule, particularly the egotistical, opt out, rather than push themselves that little bit nearer to the ultimate truth of the martial arts. All kung fu students come to this self-doubting stage and a good sifu will help them to pass through it successfully.

Direct blocks in kung fu hardly exist; if a block is made it does not stop dead upon impact. The hand keeps moving all the time, warding off rather than stopping.

■ An attack is warded off with the rear hand guard; the defender then drops onto one knee and strikes with a crippling tiger claw to the groin. In a see-saw movement, he pulls the attacker's arm downwards and at the same time strikes upwards with a palm heel to the chin.

■ Side attack 1: the defender prepares to meet the attack.

2 The attacker steps forwards with a punch.

3 Turning into the attack, the defender pre-empts the move and back-palms the oncoming punch before it has time to gain power.

4 The defender then turns into the strike she is about to deliver, thus adding more power to the knife hand to the attacker's throat.

The hand that wards off may also be used to grab an opponent, whose own strength pulls him forward and off balance. The one hand executes the two movements almost simultaneously, leaving the rearguard hand to counter any further direct attack. If none occurs, the defender is at liberty to strike at will. In executing this blocking movement, it is essential that all the weight be concentrated on the rear leg, allowing the defender to spring forward in a tiger stance, with his whole body weight behind him, if the warding and grabbing movement fails or is countered. Kung fu always has a back-up movement in readiness in case a technique fails. In kung fu one should never allow a technique to extend so far as to be impracticable. A punch should not extend so far as to throw the puncher off balance, nor should a block be carried more than six inches above the head.

One of the easiest blocks in kung fu is the 'X block', in which the practitioner crosses one wrist over the other to form a cross. This cross is then pushed upwards in the direction of the attacker's fist, which becomes trapped in the 'V' between the defender's fists. The defender's arms, still in the 'X' position, push the opponent's fist out of harm's way and then counter-attack by quickly grabbing the attacker's outstretched striking arm. The defender does this by suddenly splitting his X block and converting it to a double open-palm grab. At this stage he can either pull with both hands sharply in a downwards direction, taking the attacker to the floor, or simply twist his open-palm grab and convert it into an arm lock, thus causing the attacker excruciating pain.

In each of the sifu's lessons, he tries to teach something new but at the same time revises all the movements and self defence techniques that the students have studied so far.

KICKS AND THE USE OF THE FEET

Because kung fu is primarily concerned with hand techniques, blocks and parries, the kicking aspects of the art are left to the end of the basic training period.

The stance is the starting-point of every kung fu move, and perhaps the most obvious progression from it is a kick. Kicks will double your striking power when you have mastered them, but it must be remembered that the moment one foot is taken off the ground, the practitioner's stability and mobility are reduced by half. So that old kung fu contradiction appears yet again: by doubling his striking power the practitioner makes himself twice as vulnerable. It is for that reason that a degree of expertise is required in hand strikes and blocking techniques before a student is taught kicks.

A kick should never be attempted if there is any risk of not being able to return to a solid stance in time to parry

■ Taking the initiative 1: the attacker grabs the defender's wrist.

2 Twisting her palm inwards and then in an upward direction, the defender succeeds in turning the grab into a counter-attack.

3 The pain experienced by the attacker, as his wrist is twisted, is exacerbated when the defender adds the weight of her free arm to the technique.

4 As the attacker's body twists to the side, the defender kicks low to the joint at the back of the knee.

5 The attacker's legs give way under the pressure and he sinks to the floor.

■ Simple female self-defence techniques 1: the attacker's punch is blocked with the outer forearm.

2 This is followed rapidly by a stamp to the upper thigh.

3 The stamp is pushed, rather than kicked, into the body of the attacker.

■ Side attack 1: the defender prepares to intercept the strike.

2 The attacker's punch is halted by a chopping strike to the wrist.

3 The defender finishes the attack off with a side stamping kick to the weak point at the side of the attacker's kneecap.

■ A variation on the side attack defence 1: the attacker approaches.

2 His fist is intercepted by the forearm block, and at the same time the defender begins to lift her foot.

3 She slams it down hard in a stamping kick onto the attacker's instep.

功
夫

■ If kung fu kicks are to be effective, they must be delivered from the correct distance: if a kick falls short because it is badly timed, the kicker is placed at a disadvantage. It is therefore important that when a kick strikes home, the knee is still bent.

a counter-attack. As with hand strikes, kicks should never fully stretch the leg. A kick should be short, sharp and rapidly delivered. The usual target areas are the groin, the kneecaps or the shins.

Most kicks are executed in a sort of stomping action, the point of impact being the heel, which is the most effective weapon of the foot. In order to execute a good ankle-snap at the point of contact, a flexible and strong ankle must be developed. Another area used in attack is the ball of the foot, whose effectiveness depends upon the toes being bent back as far as possible. The ball of the foot is effective in attacks to the groin, kidneys and solar plexus. Kicking tactics in kung fu also involve the knee, which is an age-old, classic weapon for close-in fighting.

Every kick follows a simple pattern from the stance to the kick and back again to the stance. When launching a kick it is essential to be at the correct distance from an opponent. A kick which falls short places the kicker at a distinct disadvantage, because his body weight is totally behind the kick, so that it is easy for his opponent to pull him off balance. It is best to use a kicking technique as part of a larger, integrated move, combining all the basic techniques that the beginner has learned.

Having learned the basic techniques of hand strikes, blocking movements and kicks, the beginner is ready for his first test, so that he may be graded. If he is successful he is awarded a coloured sash and allowed to progress to advanced training sections. The ultimate goal is to be skilled enough in kung fu to pass the grading examination for the coveted black sash of a master. With application, this may take three to five years.

WARMING-UP EXERCISES

Before any kind of training is undergone in kung fu, the body has to be capable of muscular tasks that, for most beginners, it is not used to performing. Every training session starts with a series of health exercises. The Chinese work on the principle that to exercise the outside of the body — the arms, legs and muscles — is doing only half the job. The internal organs have to be exercised as well. The external exercises are therefore followed by internal training methods. (In recent years Western medical practitioners have been astonished by the rejuvenating properties, on the young and old alike, of these exercises.)

The warm-up is the most important part of the workout. It provides the muscles with a good supply of blood and oxygen and prepares the body for the job at hand. Never over-exercise; the ideal period should not last longer than 15 minutes.

Some points to watch out for in exercising are (1) always to be careful with the joints, (2) always to bend from the waist, never from the stomach and (3) always to keep the head looking forward, never down to the floor. The worst time to exercise is first thing in the morning, because your spine is already stretched from lying in bed all night. Lunchtime or early evening are preferable.

Kung fu has three essential elements: speed, coordination and inner strength. The specialized exercises are designed to maximize all three. Proficiency in kung fu requires that the use of the entire body, bringing into focus muscles that are seldom used in day-to-day living. Stamina, flexibility, sharp reflexes and general physical fitness are required to perform the fighting movements with ease.

The practice of kung fu requires strong legs and one of the best exercises for the legs is the horse stance. The student stands with his legs apart at about shoulders' width, sinks his abdomen low and keeps his back straight. The feet should both be pointing forward with the arms placed in front of the body, as though one were driving a car. This position should be maintained for as long as possible. At first beginners may find that after about five minutes their legs feel as though they were burning, and they may begin to shake. But it is important to push yourself to the absolute limits of your endurance. As time goes on, if the horse stance is repeated daily, you will discover that the position can be held for longer and longer as your legs become stronger.

Stretching the leg muscles and tendons increases flexibility and improves one's kicking potential, although the first purpose of stretching is to avoid injury. The muscles should be loose, so that when kicking upwards the leg is relaxed. A flexible leg allows for speed to be

■ Stretching exercises are not only useful for warming up before a training session begins, but also a very valuable contribution to good kicking techniques. Grasp the heel, and, bending the torso, push the head down to the knees. Repeat the exercise on both sides. Sit in a full splits position and lower the body gently to the floor in front. This is a potentially harmful exercise if you are not already used to stretching, so approach it with caution and never force it.

■ Waist twisting exercises: these limber up all the muscles in the upper body and thighs. Twisting should be done in a gentle, flowing manner. Overhead arm stretching exercises: these help to stretch the body from the feet right up to the neck. Squatting: lower yourself into the squatting position, without putting too much stress on the knee joint. Never bounce up and down once you are in the squatting position.

built up, thus adding power upon impact. Kicking places stress on the knee joints, the ankles, the groin and the hamstring and the muscles should always be given a chance to stretch of their own accord. During exercises one should never push, jolt, bounce or move sharply. To avoid putting undue tension on the delicate muscle structures, everything should be done smoothly.

Various methods are employed for stretching. One of the best, and probably the easiest, is to use the body weight alone. Simply allow the body to fall forward and the weight of the body will stretch your muscles. When the muscles start to tense, the stretch is beginning. If you don't feel the muscles tense, then you are not stretching at all.

One of the most commonly practised stretching exercises is the splits. The student should stand with his feet apart and gradually let each foot slide across the floor in opposite directions. The body will begin to lower towards the ground. Be careful to spread the legs, not as far as they can go, but only as far as is comfortable.

The side splits is another stretching exercise. Turn to the side, bend the front leg and place the corresponding hand on the knee of this leading leg. Extend the back leg and slide it backwards, the free hand being placed on the upper thigh of the extended leg. As the body lowers towards the ground, place the palms of both hands on the floor for support. This exercise, too, should be taken only to the comfortable stage. With time and practice full splits will be attained.

The floor scissors exercise is an all-rounder which stretches and tones up the abdomen and the whole of the lower body. The student lies on his back, raises both feet in the air and grabs each ankle at a point above the heel. He then brings in both feet so that the soles are placed in direct contact with each other. Hold this position for a second or two. Then pull each leg away in opposite directions as far as it will go. A slight strain will be felt in the abdomen and at the point where the legs join the torso.

A method for toning down after concentrating on the outside of the body, while at the same time exercising the internal organs, was invented by the old Chinese masters. It is called 'chi kung' and is a method for learning to breathe correctly. It was designed to help the individual to become stronger and healthier. The Chinese claim that, if practised regularly, it can substantially increase the body's resistance to illness.

Chi kung has no complicated movements involved and no exertion or physical force is applied to the muscles, joints or limbs. Instead, it is a method of exercising the whole of the body from within. The Eastern approach to exercise is not to thrash the body for all its worth until the person is dripping in perspiration and

■ Push-ups on one arm: this is a difficult exercise and should only be tried by the more experienced.

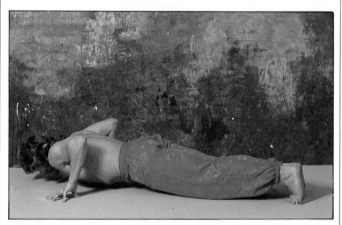

■ The basic push-up 1: this is relatively easy to perform.

2 Place the fingertips on the floor and lower the whole of the body downwards, then push the whole of the body back up, keeping the back straight. Repeat five times to begin with, and increase the number as your fitness and strength improve.

■ Advanced weapon techniques 1: the attacker attempts to strike.

2 The defender throws the closed iron fan at the attacker's wrist and follows up with a knife block.

3 The defender catches the fan in her other hand and pushes it into her attacker's throat to finish him off.

4 The force of the fan strike to the attacker's throat causes him to fall back.

aching all over. Rather, it is based on the Yoga principle, that the breath of life is everything. 'Chi' means 'vital air' and the Chinese believe that breathing exercises allow this vital air to permeate the blood, exercising along the way all the important organs of the body, including the tiny nerve cells and veins. The improved blood circulation enables practitioners to perform tasks in a more vigorous and healthy manner. The Chinese say that regular practice can increase the elasticity of the lung and heart tissues, thus improving the lung's capacity and increasing the exchange of oxygen and carbon dioxide. An additional benefit is the relief of stress and tension. In kung fu one cannot train for more than a few months without hearing the phrase 'chi kung', repeated time and time again.

The exercise begins by taking a deep breath through the nose, with the tongue placed on the roof the mouth. The air is swallowed into the lungs, the ultimate aim being to send the breath even lower, past the lungs into the stomach. Though at first this is quite hard to do, it does come with constant practice. Let the breath trickle downwards for 10 seconds. Then exhale, very gently, with the tongue placed on the bottom of the mouth. By breathing out as little as possible, more oxygen is retained in the body. This technique is done, at first, about five times, with the arms hanging limply by the sides. It should be pointed out that if a beginner is suffering from any illness he should not practise this exercise until he is well, as the sudden rush of oxygen can be harmful.

Once the general breathing has been done, the second part of the chi kung exercise begins. There are three separate exercises, done one after the other.

■ Free sparring 1: kung fu students take part in tournaments wearing protective gear. The student is gloved up and shown by the instructor how to punch.

2 A right jab to the stomach.

3 The jab is countered by the defender, who pushes downwards with her forearm.

4 She retaliates by going over the top of her partner's defence.

5 She converts her punch into an elbow strike to the face.

In the first exercise, the arms are gently rotated 35 times, first the right arm, then the left. Then the arms are raised and flicked sharply backwards. While the arms are still in the air, they make circling motions, first in a clockwise, then in an anti-clockwise direction, about 20 times. Then, suddenly, the arms are dropped down to the sides of the body again.

In the next movement, each arm is placed across the body to form a cross. This is followed by pushing the arms above the head, so that the cross breaks and the student appears to be holding up the ceiling. The arms are then allowed to drop down to the sides of the body, suddenly, as though they had become as heavy as lead.

The last of these three exercises begins by raising the legs up to waist height, keeping the back straight and the eyes looking to the front. First one leg is raised and lowered, then the other. Be careful to maintain balance at all times.

It must be remembered to breathe in (using the special breathing technique) when the arms or legs are up and to breathe out gently when they are down. Each of these exercises is done 35 times.

In quite a short time these simple exercises, though they may seem ineffective to Western minds, will reward the individual with a tremendously increased performance, both in and out of the kwoon.

ADVANCED TRAINING IN KUNG FU

After the beginner has acquired the basic principles of kung fu and enough knowledge to string together simple one- and two-step techniques, he comes into contact with what are known as 'forms'. Every martial art has its own version of forms, although they have different names. A form is a predetermined pattern of techniques that ties together proper posture, balance, coordination and timing. In practising a form, the student is taught to defend himself against a series of imaginary opponents. Every movement within a form teaches him to defend by blocking or manoeuvring and then to attack with a strike or a kick. Depending upon the style of kung fu being practised, the forms vary in length and degrees of difficulty.

The instructor will guide the beginner through each stage of the form, pointing out pitfalls along the way. Once the series of movements has been learned, the student is expected to go away and practise it day after day until he can execute each technique flawlessly and without thinking. For thought hinders reflex-action responses. In time the student will advance to more complicated forms, each devised to add extra to his training programme. Many advanced kung fu students practise

■ The instructor corrects the student's front guard defence: unless the hands are positioned correctly, all manner of counter-attacks can get through.

■ A solid defence is the hallmark of a well-taught student.

their forms blindfolded, in order to gain awareness, a sure sense of balance and the ability to react to the unexpected.

Many beginners start to practise their forms in a kind of clockwork, robotic manner. But as experience is gained through constant repetition, each movement of the form begins to flow smoothly into the next. Some kung fu clubs place a blindfolded student amid a circle of fellow students, who attack him with one technique at intermittent intervals. The blindfolded man has to pre-empt an attack as soon as he feels it coming by blocking and striking lightly in the direction that he senses it is coming from.

Kung fu training is constructed in such a way that each step is dissected by the teacher to reveal its particular function. By following a natural progression of techniques from the easy to the more difficult, the student gradually gains confidence in his capabilities. It is a slow painstaking path to technical competence, but the close mental concentration required to learn new techniques increases physical strength and as a student makes progress towards reacting instantly and harmoniously to situations, so he finds himself eager to advance further.

In advanced stages of instruction students are guided towards techniques of self-defence, under realistic conditions. This brings into play an area of training known as free sparring. Free sparring is fighting with an opponent of equal proficiency. Protective gloves and a safety helmet are worn to minimize injury. The sifu sets a time-limit to the fight, usually about two minutes, and supervises it closely. The students spar lightly, each trying to score a point by striking to a certain area of the body, employing everything he knows in his kung fu arsenal to overcome his opponent's defence and attack procedures.

■ Pak jam dao (butterfly knives): these knives are included in several kung fu systems.

■ At the advanced levels of the art, use of the butterfly knives is incorporated in a set form, or pattern.

These 'real fight' conditions, are absolutely invaluable to the student. It is here that all his shortcomings in stance, timing, speed, imagination of movement and fight strategy are highlighted.

Free sparring also teaches important lessons of self-control and distancing. Self-control is needed throughout the session, because anger will lend hostility to his fighting manner, and hostility leads to the imperfect application of fighting principles. Reflex response to blocking and striking is impaired, which results in the student lashing out wildly, with no fighting pattern, and ultimately being defeated. Sparring draws attention to misjudgements in distancing. Indeed it discloses all the faults in a student's training. The most common faults are these: (1) badly planned attacks which drain stamina; (2) poor focusing, for a hand strike or kick, on a specific target; (3) making too heavy a contact with the opponent, either

■ Sabres: fairly common kung fu weapons. The student first masters manipulation of the single sabre, then, at a more advanced level, the twin swords.

through loss of temper or misjudgement of distance; and (4) telegraphing techniques to the opponent by raising a hand or leg to strike too soon.

After the new student experiences his first free sparring fight, he returns to his daily training with an intensified ardour, determined to correct his shortcomings in order to get his fighting application up to standard for the next sparring session.

Every kung fu club conducts its training session in a programmed manner, beginning with warm-up exercises, going on to the basic techniques, and then practising forms. After that come more advanced techniques which students need to perform for the next grading.

These advanced techniques involve partnering up with a fellow student and following a step-by-step routine of attack, defence and counter-attack. A typical advanced attack might begin with one man moving in with a palm

■ A kung fu sifu, adopting the low stance and wielding the Chinese twin sabres.

strike to the sternum. The defender blocks by turning his body sideways so that the blow misses the target, and then counter-attacks with a palm-hand strike aimed upwards at the opponent's chin; this in its turn may be countered by a downwards slapping motion with a flat-palm strike to the attacker's hand and finished off with a backfist strike to the nose, using the same hand that was used to block.

Within a short space of time the student comes to a gradual understanding of the various patterns of attack. 'There is no new thing under the sun' and in kung fu the angles and arcs of attack are limited to a 360-degree area. Thus, in empty-hand combat, after all the kicks and strikes have been covered from every angle, there is nothing new with which an opponent can hit you. When this stage has been reached by the kung fu practitioner, he experiences a feeling of deep satisfaction, knowing that by constant practice every angle can be countered. His defence is therefore complete. So long as he covers every arc of attack by maintaining a good defence, he will be safe.

This is the stage to which every kung fu instructor aims to bring a student. Thereafter, all attack movements, including complicated footwork patterns, are in the hands of the student himself, to interpret as he sees fit. The student is now ready to add part of himself to his fighting capabilities. No longer does he have to follow pre-set movements. Armed with the techniques he has learned over the past months, he is free to combine them in whatever way he thinks suits his stature. A long-legged man may put more free interpretation into his kicking potential, whereas someone stocky may rely on his small size to get in close and confuse his opponent with a lightning series of hand strikes to the body.

■ The fan is an oriental accessory that can be used with great style and elegance when incorporated into one of the many kung fu forms. The sifu is using the fan in various animal stances. As has already been demonstrated, the fan can be a formidable kung fu weapon.

KUNG FU GROUND FIGHTING TECHNIQUES

Although advanced students of kung fu put techniques together for themselves, the sifu directs them in their course of self-teaching. He also instructs them in advanced forms of the system. The groundwork principles are a necessary element in the art of kung fu and they are usually taught towards the end of training, since many of them are at times contradictory to the normal rules governing training. Leaving them to the end saves confusing inexperienced students.

Although the first law of kung fu fighting states that you should, if possible, always keep two feet on the ground, circumstances arise in which a student may slip and fall to the floor, or fail to stop a strike and be knocked to the ground as a result. But even on the floor, he can still take command of a situation and turn it to his advan-

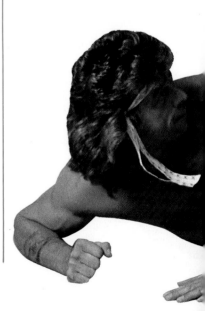

功
夫

2 When the kick is delivered, the defender ducks beneath it, well out of harm's way.

3 The attacker is now committed. The defender employs a suitable counter with a ground side-foot thrust at the attacker's groin.

■ Committing the opponent 1: the defender pre-empts an oncoming kick by dropping to the floor.

tage. An advanced student should be agile enough to be able to manoeuvre himself into any position he deems necessary, whether standing or lying on the floor.

In certain styles of kung fu, methods of combat are practised for taking someone to the ground with a sweep, called a 'take-down'. A take-down is the after-product of an initial attack. If his opponent is not standing correctly, an attacker can set him up by feinting a blow to an area of the body and following up with a sweep. Great understanding of the opponent's body movements, also of the weak points in his defence, is needed for a successful take-down. An opponent's weaknesses are usually revealed in his initial attack, which must be instantly assessed.

A typical sweep might occur in this way. An attacker throws a right punch which is blocked with an outside palm, which then wraps itself around the attacker's wrist in a grabbing movement. At the same time the defender raises his knee and pulls the attacker's extended punch aim, using that arm as a support to strike behind the attacker's kneecap with his foot. This makes the attacker fall to the floor. He is now in danger of receiving either a kick or a foot stomp. Aware of this, he spins on his back in the manner of a break dancer and the spin gives him the momentum to strike at the legs of the attacker. He

hits the standing man at a point just above the heel, bringing him to the ground.

THE TECHNIQUES OF TAI CHI CHUAN

So far we have looked at the fighting style of kung fu, from the basic procedures to the more advanced. This type of kung fu is called the 'hard style'. There is also a softer side, which has evolved far beyond the fighting form and concerns itself with psychological and physical development. It is called tai chi chuan or the 'grand ultimate fist'.

Tai chi chuan is a highly sophisticated system of self-defence, bringing together a number of skills into one form to establish a series of set principles and methods. It pays particular attention to internal strength. All movements of the tai chi chuan form are linked together in a smooth, flowing sequence. Each movement must be precisely executed. Even the smallest deviation can, as the Chinese say, 'lose you a thousand miles'.

To define the movements of the tai chi form in a short chapter is impossible. Suffice it to say that in any extended study of the martial arts it warrants closer examination. Here the form can be dealt with only briefly.

Tai chi has far fewer styles than the hand system of kung fu, only a handful in fact. The Yang style is the most popular

■ Shifting the body weight downwards 1: the attacker strikes with a palm thrust to the face. A cross-body block by the defender deflects the blow.

2 The defender ducks underneath the attack, in a low, crouching position.

3 The defender, now halfway to the floor, snakes his back foot around the attacker.

4 Using his back foot as a bar to prevent the attacker from retreating, the defender strikes with a well-timed back heel kick to the groin.

5 The sheer force of this kick sends the attacker crashing to the ground.

among Westerners, whose greatest difficulty in learning tai chi chuan has proved to be the length of its forms. Its movements relate to the four points of the compass, and a great number of movements have to be remembered. In 1956, however, a simplified version of the form was devised in China, which has helped greatly to popularize the practice of tai chi chuan in the West.

During practice the beginner should try to keep his mind calm and peaceful. The movements themselves are quite poetic and have often been likened to clouds floating in the sky. Motion is even and fluid, the muscles neither stiff nor rigid. Breathing should be deep and even, and well coordinated with opening and closing movements. The mind is tranquil but alert, its consciousness commanding the body's movements. The object is stillness in movement, a kind of unity of stillness and motion.

One of the first things required in the practice of tai chi chuan is to come to terms with its slow, dreamlike movements. Students tend to want to move faster than the form dictates. The form begins with the practitioner standing naturally, his feet shoulder-width apart and his arms hanging loosely by his side. Then very, very slowly the arms are raised to shoulder level, with the palms facing downwards. The arms then begin to lower again, palms downward, and as they press down, the knees begin to sink by bending

very slightly. From this position all the short-form movements begin and from here to the end the movement is continuous.

Tai chi chuan requires that the hands, eyes, body and limbs perform as a whole, with the legs as the base and the waist as the axis. Though the movements are gentle and slow, each part of the body is in constant motion. Practitioners should never act like a puppet; they must never focus their attention solely on the hands while neglecting the movements of the waist and legs, which are the main weight-bearing parts. The chief characteristic of tai chi chuan is that movement is initiated from a half-squatting position throughout the exercise.

In China alone there are about 250 million practitioners of the art; in the West tai chi chuan has become an aspect of medicine. On Madison Avenue in New York, the home of the great advertizing agencies, company directors and top executives have found such relief from tension by practising the tai chi form, that a permanent school has been established in the area. And reports of tai chi's beneficial effects on senior citizens in San Francisco brought this ancient martial art nation-wide acclaim. Because the form embodies so much, by doing so little, the world's senior ranking martial artists are making a serious study of it.

CHAPTER TWO

KARATE

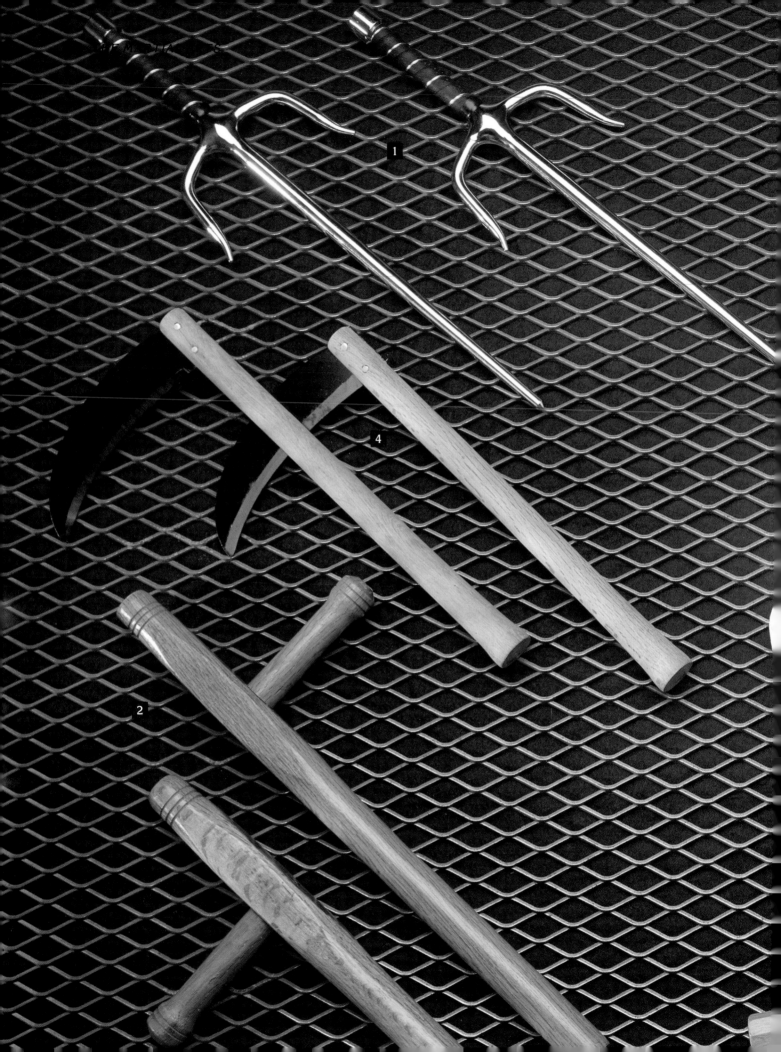

KARATE EQUIPMENT

1 The karate daggers are callad sai. 2 The pair of fighting sticks with handles are tonfa. 3 The more easily recognizable fighting sticks, joined by a short length of chain, are nunchaku. 4 The kama, as their shape suggests, were developed from the peasant's sickle. 5 The four coloured belts are kyu grades, steps on the way to the coveted shodan, the first dan black belt. The colours of the kyu belts vary according to the style of karate practised. 6 This karate suit (gi) is made of heavy duty canvas cotton. The price of a suit varies greatly, according to the cut and durability of the cloth.

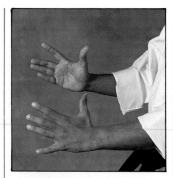

■ Making a fist 1: the correct way to clench and exercise a fist in preparation for punching.

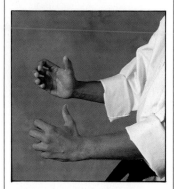

2 Bring your fingers in and wrap the thumb around the outside of the locked fingers, covering the index and second fingers.

3 The tightly clenched fist with all the air squeezed out of it: open and close each hand at least 10 times at the start of any training session to exercise the finger joints and muscles.

Karate is a Japanese form of combat that began on the island of Okinawa. The name means 'empty hands' and the art is a method of fighting which utilizes all parts of the body as deadly weapons. It consists of a series of blocks and counter-attacks by which a single exponent can render multiple assailants harmless. The art owes much to its predecessor, kung fu, which was the root of its modern development. The modern-day innovator of the system was a mild-mannered Okinawan schoolteacher named Gichin Funakoshi, who in 1917 gave a private exhibition of the art to the emperor of Japan. Impressed by what he saw, the emperor gave karate his stamp of approval and at once it became very popular. Since World War II karate has, like all the martial arts, grown at a tremendous rate. In the early 1970s an organization was established to govern karate on a world scale and to promote it as a new and fascinating sport. This organization, the World Union of Karate Organizations (WUKO), has 48 member countries.

TRAINING BEGINS

Karate has many different styles, of which the most popular throughout the world is Shotokan, meaning 'the house or club of Shoto' (Shoto was the pen name of karate's founder, Gichin Funakoshi). The place or hall where one trains is called a 'dojo'; the instructor is called a 'sensei', which is Japanese for 'teacher'. A dojo is much more than a place where a karateka (one who practises karate) trains. It is a kind of spiritual meeting place, a brotherhood of people who are all following the philosophical ways of karate as well as the physical. Therefore the dojo is treated with great reverence and respect, whether it is a room within a sports complex or simply a disused garage. All students bow upon entering and leaving. The instructor, who is always addressed as the sensei, instils principles of etiquette into every student. The strict code of conduct does much to cultivate the discipline that is so much part and parcel of karate-do ('way of karate').

Training always begins with a series of building-up and loosening-up exercises. Many schools devote almost a third of the allotted time for each lesson to these exercises. They begin with simple movement exercises such as standing with the hands on the hips and very slowly rotating the head from right to left, then reversing the procedure. This exercise relaxes the neck muscles and relieves tension. It is followed by traditional push-ups. A beginner starts with about 25 push-ups and then gradually over the following months builds the count up to 100. At one time push-ups were done on the knuckles, but since medical evidence proved that this could cause severe metacarpal damage they have been done on the

■ Basic arm stretching 1: place your finger tips in between your shoulder blades.

2 Place your other hand on your elbow, keeping both arms relaxed and your head held high.

3 Push down with the hand on the elbow, forcing your fingers to travel further down your spine. This exercise should be done at least 10 times for each arm.

空手

■ Leg strengthening 1: crouch down with your hands held behind your back and your head held high.

2 Jump up as high as you possibly can. Your thighs are doing all the work.

3 Raise your lower legs, bringing your heels up towards your thighs.

4 Try to slap your heels against your thighs as quickly as possible.

5 Straighten your legs on the descent and land on the balls of your feet. It is important not to land flat on your feet as this will jar your spine.

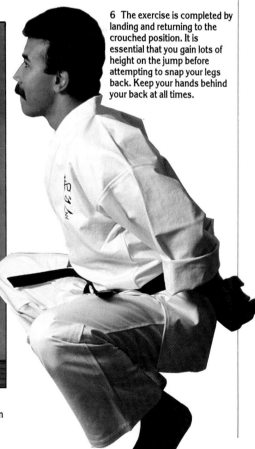

6 The exercise is completed by landing and returning to the crouched position. It is essential that you gain lots of height on the jump before attempting to snap your legs back. Keep your hands behind your back at all times.

■ Spine stretching exercise 1: these must be done slowly. Keep both legs flat and straight and gently push up with both arms. Stretch your back and at the same time look upwards. Repeat 10 times.

2 The same exercise is repeated, but this time lift your left leg up in the air, keeping it straight. Do not arch your back as much as in the previous exercise.

3 Repeat the exercise lifting your right leg. These exercises should be done at least twenty times on each leg.

■ Lie on your side with your arm outstretched above your head. Place your other arm on the floor for support and lift your leg up in the air in a scissors action. Repeat the exercise with both legs 10 times.

flat of the palms. Another typical exercise, which is aimed at stretching the legs, consists of sitting on the floor with the upper body leaning forwards and the legs wide apart and grasping an ankle with both hands. This is repeated several times on alternate legs. Some of the warming-up exercises require a partner. In one such exercise the karateka lies on his back, while the partner holds his legs, and begins a series of sit-ups. This exercise is very good for the abdomen muscles and helps to flatten a flabby stomach.

Once the exercises are finished, the formal ceremony which begins the class takes place. Everyone lines up in ranks, all facing the instructor, who is the highest authority in the dojo and is recognized by his black belt. A black belt is what is called a 'dan' grade, and signifies the level of proficiency the instructor has achieved. A dan grade can be numbered from one to ten. Traditionally speaking, once an instructor has passed all his elementary examinations and is deemed proficient, he is awarded his first dan (known as shodan). That is the first rung on the ladder of karate learning for the black belt. Before this come all the coloured belts known as 'kyu' grades. The white belt signifies an absolute beginner, whereas the brown belt indicates that the wearer is nearly ready to take his black-belt examination.

At a command given by the sensei, every member of the class shows his respect to the instructor by bowing. The students then stoop to sit on their heels and issue another formal bow before standing and beginning the lesson. Sitting on the haunches is a very important position in karate and is called 'seiza'. Once the formal etiquette is completed, the lesson begins, starting with the stance. The stances are platforms from which techniques are launched and since many of the techniques — whether strikes or blocks — require a specific stance, a thorough knowledge of all the karate stances is essential.

The first stance is the 'yoi', or the ready stance. From this position the beginner steps into the forward stance, in which about 60 per cent of the body weight is on the front or leading foot. The front leg is bent at the knee; the

空手

■ Ippon ken (one knuckle fist): the second knuckle protrudes from the fist and is used to strike soft tissue, such as the throat.

■ A lunge punch to the face: front view. The body is perfectly straight while leaning into the attack, presenting the opponent with a limited area to strike.

■ The lunge punch: side view. The toes must face the direction of the attack while the body leans forward. Look directly at your opponent.

■ Lunge punch to the groin: front view. Make sure the hip is twisted and the back leg locked straight, while leaning forward and punching to the groin.

■ Lying on your stomach, lift your lower legs and let your partner push both heels against your thighs. Repeat several times.

■ Lying on your back, keep one leg straight on the floor and lift your other leg up, bending it at the knee. Let your partner push your leg into your chest firmly and then release. Repeat the exercise several times on each leg. You must tell your partner to stop pushing if it is too painful.

■ Lying on your back, keep one leg straight on the floor and lift your other leg up, keeping it straight. Your partner, standing behind you, pulls your leg towards him gently. Repeat the exercise with the other leg.

■ Yoi stance (ready stance): standing with legs a shoulder-width apart and fists clenched in front of you.

■ Haji dachi (attention stance): standing with heels together, back straight and open hands pressed against your thighs.

■ Kokotsu dachi (back stance): this stance has 70% of the weight distributed on the back leg and 30% on the front leg, keeping both feet flat.

■ Sagi-ash dachi (crane stance): this stance has all the weight distributed on one leg. It is primarily used in katas.

■ Stance for the lunge punch: this stance is usually the first taught to the new student. The front knee is kept bent and the back leg locked straight. The punch is directed to the solar plexus of an opponent, with the left leg and left arm forward.

空手

■ Waist exercise 1: keep your legs apart and raise both arms above your head, keeping them bent at 90°. Keep your back straight and feet flat, and twist your upper body to the right.

2 Try to pivot through 180°, keeping your back straight and hands held high. Twist your body to the left and keep alternating from side to side. Repeat at least 10 times on each side.

rear leg is kept perfectly straight, with the toes turned towards the front at a 45-degree angle. The arm of the same side as the leading leg is held to the front in a punch position. The other hand, also in a clenched fist position, is tucked in against the opposite side of the body, with the thumb and fingers facing upwards. From this position most of the basic blocks and punches are executed.

In a karate punch only the first two knuckles of the fist are used to strike the target area. The fist is formed by holding the hand palm outwards, then rolling the fingers into a ball, as though they were gripping something very tightly. The thumb is pressed against the rolled-up index and middle fingers, out of harm's way. Keeping the thumb in this position gives strength to the fist and prevents the thumb from sticking out or catching on something during a fight, and fracturing or breaking.

The first punch is called the lunge punch. The karateka steps forward and, as soon as his leading leg touches the ground, throws the punch in a sort of screwing motion. The power comes from the forward movement of the entire body and the thrust from the rear leg, which is kept straight.

The punch must reach its target in a straight line, like a bullet from a gun. In karate the three possible hitting areas — from the tip of the head to the shoulders, the shoulders to the waist and the waist to the feet — are called 'jodan', 'chudan' and 'gedan'. In the early stages of learning karate, the sensei will give verbal commands in

■ Application of the elbow strike (Empi-uchi) to the mid-section; full hip twist is incorporated into the strike.

■ An elbow strike to the face, pulling the opponent onto the technique.

Japanese and the final word of each command will be the area of the body to which the technique is to be applied. A simple method for remembering the names of the three areas is to associate them with a particular point of the body. Since 'chudan' is the middle area, remember *chu* for 'chest'. 'Gedan' being the lower area, *ge* can stand for 'guts'. That leaves only 'jodan' for the head.

Possibly the most commonly used punch in karate is the reverse punch. In most competitions, this reverse punch or 'gyaku-zuki' as it is known, scores more points than any other technique. A beginner should therefore concentrate on perfecting it very early on. The reverse punch is also the strongest and hardest punch in karate. The reverse punch is most frequently used in a counter-attack. The incoming fist of an opponent is blocked by a simple rising block and then quickly countered with a gyaku-zuki. This is delivered by punching with the opposite hand to the leading leg. A twisting thrust of the hip, thrown into the forward movement of the body, adds to the power of the attack.

As the karateka strikes, his other hand is pulled back sharply. This not only adds power to the punch, but also gives the karateka a second strike in readiness, should it be needed. The punch can be directed to any target area.

The simple block just mentioned, the rising block, is one of the first two blocks a beginner learns. It protects an incoming punch from around the waist upwards. The other block, the downward block, protects from the waist to the feet and is essential to stop kicks hitting the body.

One of the leading principles of karate is that an attack should be met halfway, before the strike gains power. If a punch is aimed at the face, the defender steps out to intercept it before it gains momentum. The block, executed in an upwards twisting motion of the arm, prevents the strike from hitting the intended target, while the attacker, his punch now way off course, is left vulnerable to a counter-strike. The downward block, used against kicks, is executed with the student standing in the ready stance.

If an opponent kicks, say to the groin area, the defender steps forward, accelerating from the rear foot, which then becomes the leading foot. The arm on the same side as that foot is then brought across the centre of the body before striking downwards. The hand can be either a clenched fist or an open palm, depending upon how the defender wishes to counter attack. The force of the block sends the attacker spinning around, and frequently he ends up with his back to the defender, thus presenting the defender with a perfect opportunity to deliver a counter-strike to the kidneys, a vulnerable area unprotected by bone.

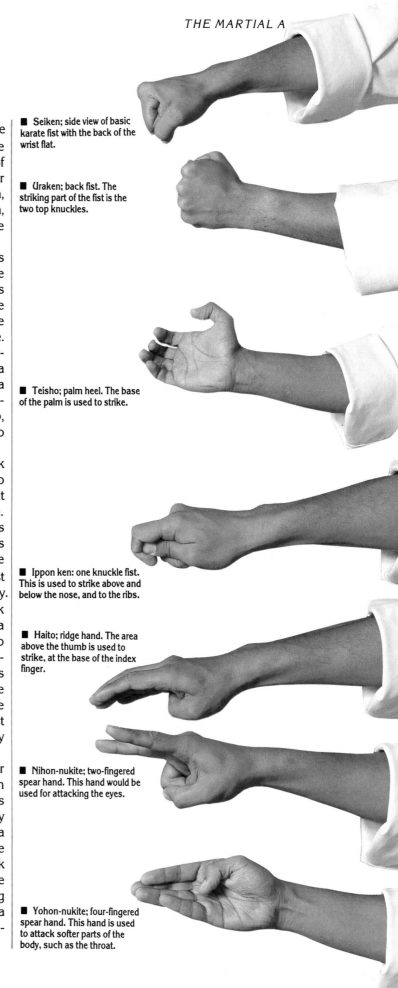

■ Seiken; side view of basic karate fist with the back of the wrist flat.

■ Uraken; back fist. The striking part of the fist is the two top knuckles.

■ Teisho; palm heel. The base of the palm is used to strike.

■ Ippon ken: one knuckle fist. This is used to strike above and below the nose, and to the ribs.

■ Haito; ridge hand. The area above the thumb is used to strike, at the base of the index finger.

■ Nihon-nukite; two-fingered spear hand. This hand would be used for attacking the eyes.

■ Yohon-nukite; four-fingered spear hand. This hand is used to attack softer parts of the body, such as the throat.

■ 1 Both karate-ka are in the left fighting stance.

2 The defender on the right pushes off his right leg, preparing to counter.

3 The defender counters with a reverse punch to the attacker's stomach. Full hip twist is used when the punch is delivered.

■ Sparring mitts, which are compulsory for any form of competition, minimize the risk of injury to the face.

■ From this view you can see how the padded mitts cover the whole of the knuckle area.

空手

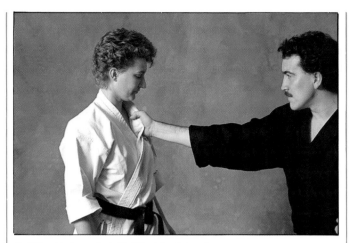

■ 1 The attacker grabs hold of the defender's collar with his right hand.

2 The defender quickly grabs the attacker's hand with her right hand.

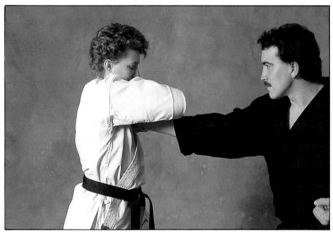

3 The defender turns his palm upwards, twisting her body to the right in the process.

4 Placing her left forearm against his elbow joint, the defender applies pressure downwards.

5 Continuing the pressure, the defender forces her attacker to the floor.

6 Once the attacker's elbow is locked, it is very difficult for him to counter.

7 He ends up in a weak position, open to many follow-up techniques.

■ Application of the wrist lock 1: both thumbs are pressed into the back of the attacker's hand, forcing the wrist back on itself.

2 With such pressure being applied, the attacker is easy to control.

3 Once the attacker is down, he is at the defender's mercy.

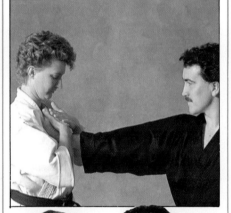

■ 1 The attacker grabs the defender's collar with his right hand.

2 The defender places both hands, palms inwards, on the back of the attacker's hand, pressing firmly inwards.

4 Continuing to lean forward, the defender forces the attacker down to the ground.

3 The defender then leans forward, forcing the attacker's fingertips and wrist backwards.

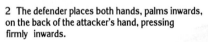

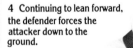

5 Once the attacker is down, a follow-up technique is easily applied.

空手

LEARNING THE KICKS

The use of kicks is what chiefly distinguishes karate from Western boxing. A kick is stronger than a punch and has a much greater reach. A little man, faced with a much larger adversary, can compensate for his opponent's longer arm reach by using his legs as defensive weapons. The karate repertoire has a vast array of technical kicks. At the beginner's level, it is deemed sensible that the student isn't confused by their many names. Beginners concentrate on the basic four: the front kick, the side kick, the back kick and, perhaps the most powerful of all, the roundhouse kick.

THE FRONT KICK

The front kick, more correctly called the front snap kick, is delivered from the forward stance with the rear foot. The rear foot is used because it has the forward thrust of the body behind it. The foot is brought up to waist height, then quickly snapped out in a thrusting motion. At first a beginner learns this kick in a one-two-three rhythm, but as proficiency increases the whole movement becomes one smoothly flowing action. The toes of the kicking foot should be curled outwards to avoid injury, impact being made with the ball of the foot. This kick is usually aimed at a fleshy area of the body. After delivering the kick, the foot must be pulled back very quickly and brought back down to the ground to leave the karateka in his original stance. While the kick is being executed the hands should always maintain a good, high-guard position, as a defence against a counter-strike should the kick be blocked or misdirected.

THE SIDE KICK

The side kick is a very good kick to use against areas of the body with a hard bony consistency, such as the knees, although it may be directed at any area of the body. This kick may be very fast, but it can be detected by an opponent much earlier than many other kicks in karate. It is effective chiefly in defence, since in delivering it the karateka presents only the side of his body to his opponent, thereby protecting all his vital areas.

The part of the foot used in the strike can be either the edge or the heel. The power comes from the thrust of the hip. The kick is executed by bringing the kicking foot up to the knee of the supporting leg. The leg is then snapped outwards, with the hips behind the thrust. The upper part of the body leans in the direction of the kick. The kicking leg is never quite fully extended, in order to prevent injury to the knee joint and to facilitate a fast withdrawal. After the kick is executed the kicking foot is brought back to the level of the supporting leg's knee and then down to the floor.

THE ROUNDHOUSE KICK

The roundhouse kick uses either the instep or the ball of the foot as a weapon. This particular kick, unlike most of the basic kicks, does not travel in a straight direction, but takes a sideways, half-circular movement, rising from the ground and continuing in an arc to the target area. It is spectacularly fast and extremely powerful.

Most beginners find that the roundhouse kick is the most difficult to learn. It can be easily executed from either the leading foot or the back foot, but a roundhouse kick delivered from the rear leg is the more powerful, it

■ The front kick 1: adoption of the left stance, ready to deliver the kick.

2 The back supporting foot is brought forwards and raised with the knee bent.

3 The leg is extended and kicked outwards, the hips are pushed into the kick and the toes are bent well back.

4 The leg is snapped back very quickly with the knee kept at the same height.

5 The leg is then returned to the floor, in readiness for any counter-attack.

■ The side kick 1: taking up the left stance.

2 Raising the right leg and bending at the knee, twist slightly to the left.

3 The side kick thrusts into the opponent's body.

■ In the left stance 1: step forward, bringing the right foot to the front .

空
手

2 Raise the right knee.

3 Twist on the ball of the supporting foot, bringing the hips around through 90°.

4 Extend the right leg, striking with the instep of the foot.

■ Application of the roundhouse kick to the head with the left leg.

■ Application of the back roundhouse kick to the head (above), using the right heel. Application of the sidekick to the mid-section (below).

has more time to gather speed. The hips turn further, too — and this hip turn makes it difficult for the beginner to keep his balance.

The kick is performed by starting from a natural stance and bringing up the right leg, bent and to the side. The karateka then pivots halfway round on the ball of the left foot, while rotating the entire body forward. As the kick travels through the arc of attack, the knee is snapped just before the foot hits the target. The hands should maintain a guard position throughout the manoeuvre. When the kick is completed, the foot is drawn back to the starting position. It is not unusual to see a karate expert execute a roundhouse kick to his opponent's head. This is done by bringing the foot back to the starting position and then striking again equally quickly with the same foot, either to another area of the body or at the opponent's legs, behind the upper heel, to sweep him to the ground. In karate terminology this is known as a combination technique.

THE BACK KICK

The back kick is more of a thrusting kick than an actual kick in itself. It is usually performed from a fighting stance and is most useful against attacks from more than one opponent. The common mistake of beginners in delivery of this kick is to let their guard drop; the primary aim of the kick is to disable an enemy who is attacking from behind, while at the same time keeping guard against a frontal attack from someone else.

In executing the movement the kicking foot is brought up to knee level of the supporting leg, which should be slightly bent. The karateka then glances over his shoul-

空手

■ The back kick 1: take up the left stance.

2 Pull the left leg across the body to the right and pivot on the balls of the feet through 180°.

3 Raise the right leg so that the knee comes up to the chest.

4 Extend the right leg outwards, pulling the toes back sharply so that you strike with the heel to the chest area.

der in the direction the kick is going to travel — the look should be only a very quick glance, not a prolonged stare. Once the target is located, the kicking leg is thrust at it in a straight line. The eyes must not linger to examine what damage has been caused. It is sufficient to know that the immediate danger from the rear has been cancelled out. Efforts should then be entirely concentrated on the frontal attack.

These, then, are the four basic kicks. Students will be expected to have a thorough knowledge of them for their first grading exam. To help the beginner learn these basic techniques, there are solo exercises, called 'katas'.

THE KARATE KATA ('THE SOUL OF KARATE')

The karate kata is a carefully devised procedure for teaching a beginner how to flow from one technique into another without a break. It was designed by the old masters to allow for the aesthetic development of the practitioner. It teaches correct stances and breathing and it emphasizes coordination and timing. Its series of choreographed fighting movements includes all the techniques required to deal with almost any situation and it allows the student to display his competence of the art to its maximum. The modern founder of karate, Gichin Funakoshi, regarded the karate kata as the very soul of the art. To the outsider the movements of a kata resemble a dance routine.

All beginners have to learn the katas, the names of which differ according to the style of karate being prac-

tised. The first basic katas are usually called 'heian' or 'pinan' katas. The student needs to immerse himself in the performance of a kata in order to release his emotions. He must think in terms of thousand upon thousand of repetitions when practising a particular kata, for only through constant repetition will he be able to master the basic fighting movements and to achieve the physical and spiritual sensitivity that lies at the heart of the martial arts. Only then will he have gained complete control over all parts of his body. Once that level of proficiency has been achieved, the kata takes on a new meaning. While performing the required movements within the kata, the student is able to meditate. A kata performed at this level has been called 'moving Zen'. At this stage of his development the karateka seems to be able to sense the movements of his opponents before they occur, enabling him to react with blinding speed and absolute control.

It takes great discipline and hours and hours of practice to perfect just one kata and many beginners soon lose interest. The kata is a test of personal endurance and the dedicated practitioner will overcome the boredom stage to look deeper into its hidden meaning. He will not only develop the lightning reactions and instincts that are the hallmark of karate champions, but will follow the path of karate-do for life.

An instructor begins teaching kata to his class by making each movement clear and concise. Students, at first, have to follow every intricate movement mechanically. A good instructor will explain at every stage what each technique, when applied under real circumstances, is capable of. In this way the students become aware that each movement of the kata has a specific purpose, and knowing that makes it easier to remember the kata sequences. The student's attention to correct stance, breathing and arm movement must be constant in order to avoid the slide into bad habits, which may be difficult to correct at a later stage.

After about a dozen movements have been learned, they are strung together in a kata sequence and practised over and over again before going on to the next set of kata movements. All beginners are required to master the first kata before taking their first grading examination.

THE FIRST BELT GRADING EXAMINATION

Once the primary movements have been learned — the stances, kicks, punches and blocks — and also a first kata, a new student is required to take an examination, called a grading. The successful candidate is awarded his next kyu grade. This is a coloured belt, which signifies that its owner is eligible to take the next step on the rung

■ Kata movement followed by its application 1: from the kick block position.

2 Step forward with a right lunge punch to the body.

3 Application of the downward block.

空手

■ The right stance 1: the opponents consider possible angles of attack.

2 The attacker strikes with a left thigh kick, using his lower shin.

3 Continuing with the kick, he uses it to sweep his opponent.

4 Application of the lunge punch.

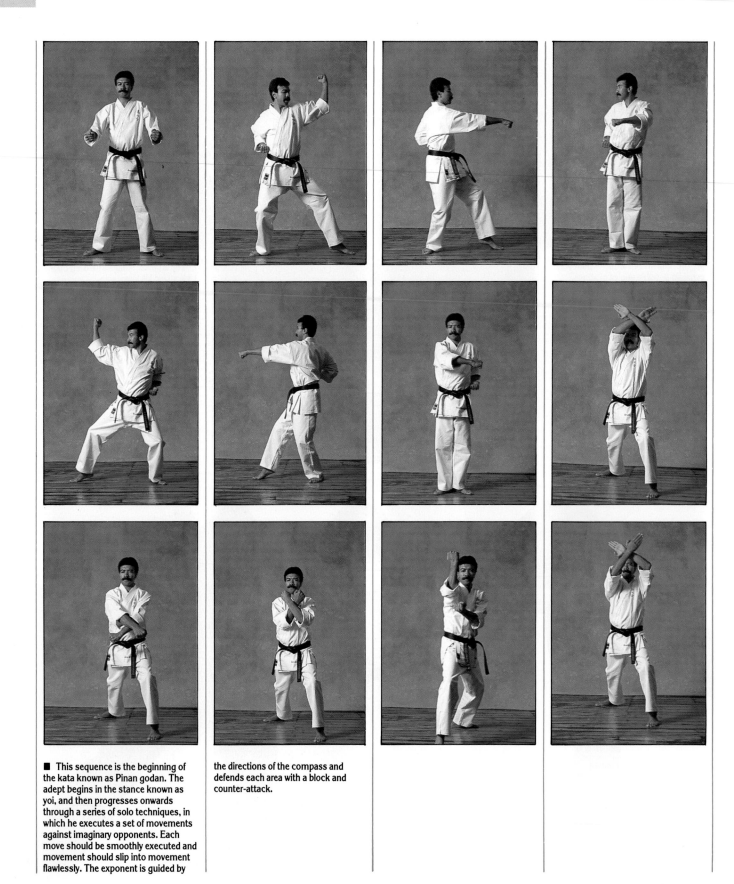

■ This sequence is the beginning of the kata known as Pinan godan. The adept begins in the stance known as yoi, and then progresses onwards through a series of solo techniques, in which he executes a set of movements against imaginary opponents. Each move should be smoothly executed and movement should slip into movement flawlessly. The exponent is guided by the directions of the compass and defends each area with a block and counter-attack.

空手

■ Application of the right inside block 1: against a reverse punch.

2 The defender applies a backfist counter-attack directly after the block.

up the ladder to karate proficiency. The frequency of gradings varies from club to club, but generally they are held once every three months.

The first grading is very important, since it gives the sensei the opportunity to assess how each new student performs under examination conditions. He will not expect miracles, only a reasonable standard of proficiency. The grading curriculum consists of only the basic techniques that have been learned so far. No surprise movements are suddenly introduced.

All commands to perform techniques are given in the Japanese language. This is standard throughout the world, not only because of tradition, but because of the number of international karate competitions that take place. If no standardized language were used at an international tournament, with referees, judges, timekeepers and competitors from all over the world, utter confusion would reign. Many beginners find it difficult, at first, to remember the Japanese phrases, but within the first few months of practice the language barrier begins to fade at a rapid rate.

During the grading examination students take the middle of the floor either singly or in groups of three, depending upon the total number being graded. Impeccable etiquette is required from everyone; discipline and good manners, have to be observed at all times. All the bows and correct responses are taken into account in

■ The double outside block 1: in this situation, the attacker is in the left stance, the defender in the right.

2 The attacker lunges out to grab the defender's throat with both hands, who in turn prepares to execute a double outside block.

■ The single outside block 1: against a reverse punch.

assessing the overall grading marks. Successful candidates — and very few students fail the first grading — are promoted to the next kyu grade. This is usually the 7th kyu, denoted by a yellow belt, but this may vary from club to club. Once the first grading has been successfully completed, the student goes on to the next stage of training, which concerns itself with basic semi-free sparring.

SEMI-FREE SPARRING

Semi-free sparring involves the beginner in an actual fighting situation under controlled conditions. It is introduced to complement the basic blocks, punches and stances already learned and consists of a series of attacking and defensive moves, decided upon beforehand, which help the karateka to train and sharpen his reflexes. The specific term used for such an exercise is 'one-step semi-free sparring'. Two students face each other, one as the attacker, the other as the defender against an attack which he knows is coming. To the outsider it may look somewhat robotic in its execution; but each technique that is performed helps to familiarize the students with real conditions under fire.

As an example, let us suppose that the incoming attack is a punch to the sternum, or upper chest. The attacker adopts the forward stance, with a clenched fist held above the thigh in a low block position (gedan barai). His other hand remains in the traditional ready stance, fist clenched, resting by the hip. The defender stands in the ready position (yoi), awaiting the impending attack. The attack begins with the attacker taking one full step forward and punching outwards with his 'cocked' fist, that is, the one that was resting on the hip. When the

空手

3 The defender forces the attacker's arms apart and prepares to strike with her leg.

4 She drives her left knee into his chest to immobilize him.

2 The defender follows through with a left reverse punch to the kidney.

■ The double sweep 1: both fighters square off in the right stance.

2 The attacker sweeps with his left leg.

3 Continuing the sweep, he follows through, placing his opponent off balance.

4 The attacker places his left leg down and pivots through 180° to the right, extending his right leg.

5 Dropping onto his left knee, the attacker sweeps the supporting leg of his opponent with his own right leg.

6 A successful take-down is completed.

7 The attacker's right leg is then snapped back and kicks to the body of the downed opponent.

空手

■ Types of strike 1: The attacker steps forward into the right stance to deliver a right lunge punch. The defender side-steps, blocking with his left forearm.
2 The defender prepares to counter, using his left arm.

3 Jumping in quickly behind the attacker, the defender uses his left arm for a backfist strike to the rib cage.

4 Pulling his left fist back, the defender prepares to strike to the same target area with his right arm.

5 Twisting his hip fully to the right, the defender strikes with a right ridge hand to the ribs.

defender sees the attack coming, he steps back smartly and at the same time raises his hand to execute an inside block. (By stepping back as he blocks, he doubly protects himself: even if the block fails, he has distanced himself from the oncoming punch.) The inside block is akin to a man drawing a sword with his right hand from a scabbard on his left side. The block knocks the oncoming punch off course and completely exposes the attacker's frontal area.

The defender now turns attacker, stepping quickly forward and striking with a reverse punch to his attacker's chest. The punch is executed with his left hand, which will have been resting in 'hammer' at the side of his hip. As the punch strikes the target area or, correctly speaking, just an inch short of the area — in karate, no actual full-power blows are landed on the opponent's body — the defender emits a loud shout or yell. This is termed the 'kiai', or super-power shout. The shout is made as the defender strikes, exhaling sharply.

KIAI – THE YELL OF SUPER-POWER

The sounds of loud yells and weird shouts emanate from martial arts dojos around the world. Non-practitioners commonly associate these sounds with the breaking of wood or other materials. This is near the truth, but the kiai, for which there is no adequate English translation, is much more than 'just a shout'. Virtually all the Japanese martial arts use it as a means of producing extra power from within the body — just as weightlifters make great grunting and groaning noises when attempting a particularly heavy lift. In World War II American servicemen who parachuted out of aeroplanes screamed the name 'Geronimo' as a war cry, perhaps to give them added incentive to jump from a great height, and the karate kiai has something of this in it, too.

In karate the kiai is used during the execution of a focused technique. Done correctly, and at the right time, it can add power to the technique being performed. A kiai harnesses the body's energy and allows it to escape by an aggressive exhalation of breath, either just before or during an attack. Moreover, if it is applied at the instant before the actual strike goes in, the loud, shrill sound has the effect of momentarily stunning an opponent, and in that brief fraction of a second a whole range of techniques can be directed towards a target. In this way the kiai can give a person an edge.

Beginners learn the kiai right from the outset of their training. During the 'kihon' exercises (basic training in class), the whole club practises punching and blocking in long lines, moving down the hall until space runs out. At that point the sensei commands them to turn, with the order 'mawatte'. The class turns in unison and every member exhales powerfully, using the kiai shout to do so. The kiai originates from the diaphragm, thus using the muscles of the lower chest and stomach, the strong contraction of which forces the air out of the lungs.

Many beginners are at first baffled as to how to make the shout. Some shout it very loudly, while others emit a sound resembling the 'aaaaah' of a man falling from a skyscraper. By the time they reach brown belt level, however, the kiai should be resembling the sound of a very loud and strenuously emitted 'its'.

THE TRAINING CONTINUES

As the beginner progresses to more advanced areas of basic training, the simple blocks give way (though they are not discarded) to more demanding techniques. These are known as combination techniques, which teach a karateka to assemble basic movements in a series, or pattern, which may be used for defence or attack. By creating a tactical fighting mode, the beginner is able to change his approach, if necessary, for instance, if his first attack is stopped by a block. After an efficient counter-attack, which may have been instigated as a ruse, the attacker can move in on another area of his target, one that may be wide open for an effective technique. Care must always be taken, of course, because his opponent may purposely have left the area open to provoke just such an attack. Combination techniques between two adversaries are pretty much tit for tat, the outcome depending upon which fighter has the quickest reactions, the finest timing, the best execution of techniques and the most efficient plan of attack.

Combination attacks strike with a series of techniques from different angles and directions. The object is to find a gap in the opponent's defences. When that gap is found, the attacker exploits it by unleashing a rapid barrage of kicks and punches to score points.

The beginner normally learns combination techniques by performing them against thin air. Once he is able to execute a few of them, he tests them on a punching-bag, which will give him an indication of the impact power each technique possesses.

The variety of combination techniques, using all the basic movements, is endless. A typical example is as follows. The two partners face each other. The attacker moves forward in a left fighting stance with a front kick off the right leg to the groin area. As he kicks, he changes his hand-guard position in readiness for a counter-attack. After the kick is executed, he returns the leg that has kicked it to the ground and immediately follows up with a roundhouse kick off the opposite leg, using the front leg as a support. The roundhouse kick is aimed at

■ Free fighting techniques 1: the attacker prepares to deliver a front kick.

2 The defender blocks downwards to stop the kick.

空手

punch is an ideal technique to use at close quarters. Both fighters have to be in left fighting stances, at the correct range, for it to be applied correctly. The attacker punches forwards with a rapid, sharp jab, executed off the leading fist and utilizing a forward lean of the body, which gives the punch its strength. If the first punch is effectively blocked, then the attacker moves in nearer and unleashes the other fist.

The backfist, although not a completely controlled technique, since difficulty arises in judging its strength and speed, is especially effective at short range. It is delivered with a whiplash action with the knuckles of the hand. The wrist must be pliant and completely relaxed. The area struck is usually the face. Because of the high speed with which it is executed, it is a very difficult technique to block.

Exploration of karate techniques continues with open-handed blocking methods, more elaborate kicks and head height (jodan) and when it is completed, a final kick — the back kick — is performed. As the last kicking leg returns to the ground, the body will tend to incline towards the side, presenting a side view to the opponent. The attacker then turns his body in a half-circle while he raises his right leg, using the left leg for support. The right leg is raised to about knee height and is then thrust sharply backwards at the opponent. It is important that at the moment of execution the attacker looks into the kick to note its direction, while maintaining a high-guard position with his hands. The hands will also act as a stabilizer for balance.

The next stage of learning involves more stances and punching routines. Two favourite techniques in competition are the snap punch and the backfist. The snap

advanced sweeping techniques. All the time the karate arsenal of weapons is building up, giving the karateka an overall view of the means at his disposal to mount an attack or sustain a defence. Many karate movements suit certain individuals more than others. A tall student with very long legs may well be drawn to the kicks, whereas a small person may prefer close-in fist strikes. Each individual achieves his own style by trial and error. What works for one person may not suit another. Continual training in the basic movements and adapting them to one's own requirements is required.

Once a certain level of proficiency has been reached, the karate student starts to learn stances beyond the basic stance. One of these is the famous 'cat stance', which is a natural development from the basic stance. The position places virtually all the weight of the body on the back, or supporting, leg. From the natural stance, the front foot moves a little farther out from the body and into line with the rear foot. The rear leg bends at the knee, supporting all the body weight. The front leg also bends at the knee, with the heel raised from the ground so that only the ball of the foot touches the floor (a sort of tip-toe position). A common fault experienced by most karatekas in the early stages of learning this stance is to allow the body to fall forward because not enough weight has been concentrated on the back leg. The cat stance is an ideal stance from which to execute a front snap kick.

Another more advanced stance is the free-fighting stance. In fact, since free fighting changes all the time to meet new circumstances and requirements, the stances also change at a rapid pace. But at the beginning of a match, whether at club or national level, the accepted basic stance is this free-fighting one.

3 The attacker now has his back to the defender.

4 The defender prepares to strike to the kidneys.

The fighter usually places his body at a 45-degree angle and distributes his weight equally on both feet, with the knees slightly bent. He is thus able to move from one stance into another very quickly, and the angled position of the body narrows the target offered to his opponent.

FREE-FIGHTING COMPETITION

One of the main purposes of karate training is to enable the student to use the techniques he has learned in either self-defence or active competition. The self-defence side of the art is perhaps self-explanatory. Competition simulates real combat, only with rules and regulations. There comes a time when a karateka wishes to test himself against his peers. This stage of training is catered for by inter-club competitions.

The first taste of free fighting with an opponent, under a system that requires the individual to make his own decisions as to which techniques to use, can seem somewhat daunting. It is a test of personal ability; there are no winners or losers.

In the period leading up to the actual fight, first-time fighters are suddenly stricken with nervous tension. Self-doubt creeps in and negative thoughts cloud the mind — 'will I get hurt? how will I know what technique to use? will I make a fool of myself?' But every great competition fighter has asked himself those very questions. Pre-fight nerves afflict virtually everyone. When a fighter actually gets on to the mat, the self-doubts seem to vanish and the mind concentrates upon the job at hand. This is the reward for hours of basic training. Those long months spent on repetitive practice of techniques pay off. The fighter goes out and his reflexes take over. The opponent may move in and strike with a roundhouse kick to the head and the first-time fighter may not actually see it coming. But pure, instinctive reaction moves his body out of harm's way.

A free-fighting match is held under strict rules. Any action that might harm an opponent is forbidden. Although the kicks and punches are released with great intent, the actual strikes fall just short of the target areas. Judging such a fast-paced event requires great skill, and it is necessary to have highly qualified referees and judges to evaluate each technique and award scoring points. Although a standardized set of rules has been formulated by WUKO, karate associations in countries outside their jurisdiction do not have to abide by them. For this reason a certain amount of confusion about the scoring system has arisen in recent years. Be that as it may, it is safe to say that no matter which rules a karateka fights under, he will get a fair deal.

Before a fight begins it is extremely important that the fighters express respect for each other and for the officials judging them. This is done with a formal bow. The two fighters then stand at attention awaiting instructions to begin. A positive mental attitude is needed by each fighter at this point. If a fighter's expression were to show fear, or if he were to appear nervous, his opponent would take advantage of his lack of confidence during the fight. Waiting for the signal to begin, the fighter should therefore look confident and sharp.

At the referee's signal the fighters begin. To score

■ Unbalancing the opponent 1: the attacker and defender are in the left stance.

■ The left free fighting stance.

■ The cat stance; front view.

2 The cat stance; side view. The ball of the front foot is in contact with the floor and 80% of the body weight is supported on the back leg.

空手

■ Application of the roundhouse block 1: the attacker grasps the defender's neck with both hands, who pushes both arms upwards through the grip to break the hold.

2 The defender crosses his hands, placing his right hand underneath the attacker's right arm and his left hand on top of the defender's left arm.

3 The defender, moving both his arms in a clockwise direction, twists the attacker's arms around.

4 Completing the roundhouse block, he locks arms.

2 The attacker attempts a right front kick. The defender sidesteps and extends the attacker's kicking leg forward with her left leg, unbalancing him.

3 She then counters with a right reverse punch to the attacker's right kidney.

■ The attacker throws a right front kick 1: the defender sidesteps and jumps forward, punching with his right hand to the body and preparing to grab the kick.

2 The defender grabs the leg and unbalances the attacker.

3 The defender steps up with his left leg, lifting the attacker's leg even higher, and sweeps the attacker's supporting leg away from him with his right leg.

4 The attacker is lifted into the air.

5 The defender controls the attacker's descent so that his opponent is placed directly in front of him.

6 The defender slams the attacker onto his back.

7 The defender pins the attacker down with his left knee.
8 He then counters with a left reverse punch to the face.

空手

points, the techniques must be cleanly performed and strongly focused at the appropriate target areas. To win a match the contestant must score three full points, which are called 'ippons', or six half-points, called 'wazaris'. If neither contestant has scored three full ippons at the end of the match, the victory is awarded to the fighter with the most points scored. Recently safety regulations have made it obligatory for all competitors to wear fist protectors. A special guard for the leg, known as a shin protector, is optional, as are groin guards and gumshields.

■ COMPETITION TACTICS ■

The first-time fighter arriving on the competition scene has only a limited number of techniques. His 'game plan' will therefore be something of a trial-and-error affair. The

new fighter will move around the area looking for openings in his opponent's defence. Seizing the opportunity at the right moment, he will link together a series of strikes, probably involving kicks, in an attempt to break through and score points. At this moment he is most vulnerable to a counter-attack. The seasoned fighter would be well aware of this and would take precautionary countermeasures. Tactical manoeuvring and the ability to 'read' a fight come with experience.

Competition fighting can perhaps be likened to a game of chess; a player only improves by continually playing against another chess player better than himself. In karate, once a grasp of workable techniques have been thoroughly practised. The karateka can try them out, at first on students at his own level. Then later, as his speed and timing improve and after gaining a certain amount of success over his own ranks, he can go a step

■ Coming out on top 1: the attacker and defender both assume the right stance.

2 The attacker lunges forwards with a left stomach punch; the defender sidesteps, and executes a right inside block.

3 The defender grabs the attacker's outstretched left arm, pulling it past him, striking simultaneously with a right knife hand to the throat.

4 Pushing her arm against the attacker's chest, the defender leans backwards, breaking the balance of the attacker.

5 They fall backwards: the defender's fall is broken by the attacker's arm, which is damaged upon impact with the floor.

- A right ridge hand strike to the throat.

- A right backfist to the temple.

■ The application of techniques 1: the attacker and defender both begin in the right stance.

2 The attacker prepares to sweep the defender with his left leg.

3 The attacker sweeps the defender's right leg away, totally unbalancing him.

4 With the defender's back to him, the attacker prepares to throw a reverse punch.

5 The defender quickly grasps the attacker's left arm; his left wrist grasps the attacker's wrist, his right hand grabbing the shoulder.

6 Pulling the attacker's arm towards him, the defender sweeps the attacker's left leg with his right leg.

7 The defender then follows up with a reverse punch to the spine.

8 The defender pulls back the fist ready for a second strike, should it be necessary.

空手

higher and spar with a student with more experience than himself.

Complicated techniques almost never work in serious competition; the simple ones work every time. Most of today's great tournament fighters on the world circuits limit themselves to a few techniques that work best for them. Probably the most effective and most common scoring technique in karate is the gyaku-zuki, or reverse punch, which the beginner learns in the second week of his basic training, and provides a good illustration of the need constantly to return to practising the basics. However boring they seem to become, they are the roots of the art.

Competition techniques are pretty much down to the individual himself. But there are certain tactical guidelines one can follow. Modern tournament fighters keep on the move all the time. They do not wait to be hit. Constant movement makes it easier both to initate attacks and to defend against them. Light, free manoeuvrability also helps to avoid the telegraphing of techniques to an opponent. The area in which the fight is taking place should be exploited to the maximum. Inexperienced fighters are apt to stay in the centre all the time, making it easy for an opponent to strike, as it is nearly akin to hitting a statue. On the other hand, it is important to avoid being pushed into a corner. Not only is your freedom to defend against attack greatly restricted, but if you step out of the permitted fighting area you will be penalised. Another rule is to avoid heavy contact, however accidental, with the opponent's body, as this will incur penalties or disqualification.

A typical example of a tactical competition manoeuvre is as follows. The fighters face each other in the typical free-fighting stance, each with his left foot forward. The attacker moves in with a roundhouse kick to the head and the defender raises his arm to ward it off. As soon as the block is instigated, the attacker switches his attack by bringing his right leg down into a sweep position, directly behind the defender's leading foot. He hooks his leg forward and sweeps his opponent to the ground, finishing him off with a reverse punch to the head. Hundreds of different combinations exist on this theme. It is up to the karateka to explore as many as possible.

A FINAL NOTE

Throughout a beginner's training, many obstacles are raised. The key is perseverance, coupled with unstinting practice. Karate has quite a high drop-out rate because of the hard work involved and the constant repetition of techniques. The principles of karate training are not just about fighting: karate is about developing character, finding out about oneself. To harmonise mind and body, this is the true essence of karate-do: the empty hand way.

■ Application of techniques 1: the attacker and defender square off, both in the left stance.

2 The attacker prepares to kick the defender's guard down.

3 A right crescent kick to the defender's leading hand.

4 Following through with the assault, the attacker places his right foot forward.
5 The attacker throws a right reverse punch to the defender's kidneys.

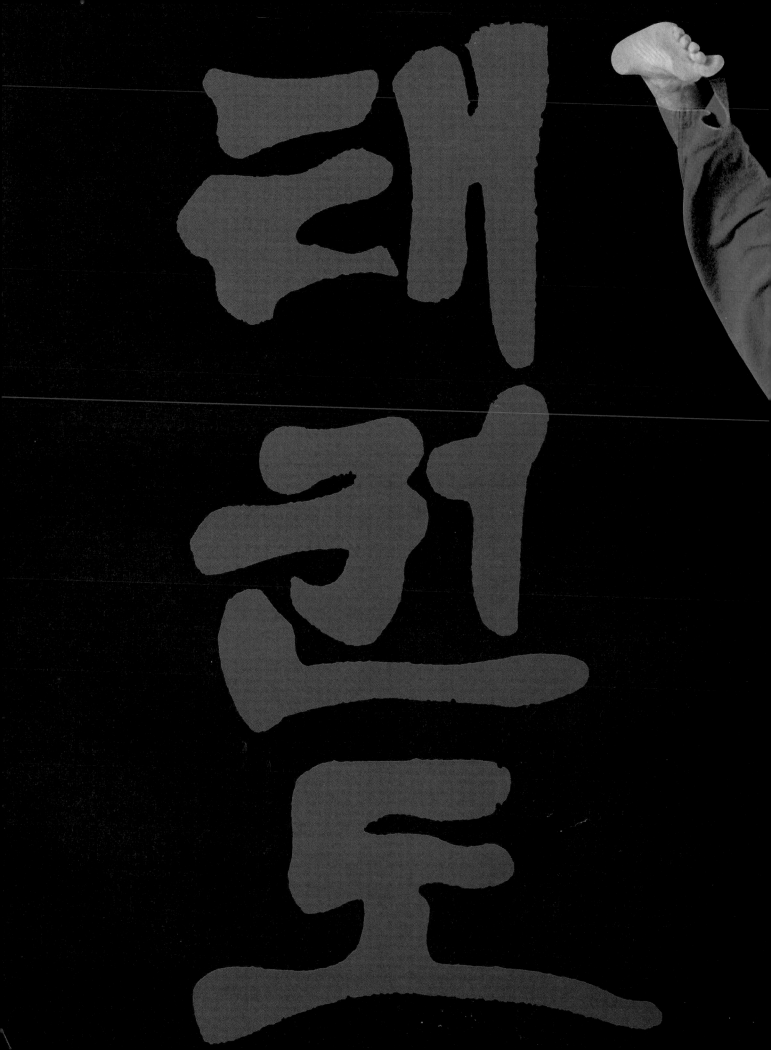

CHAPTER THREE

TAEKWONDO

SUPERMASK

4

3

SUPERSHIN

SUPERSHIN

TAEKWONDO EQUIPMENT

Specific weapons are not associated with taekwondo. 1 The taekwondo suit is called a tobok; like the other martial arts uniforms, it is loose-fitting and has developed from the peasant's costume. 2 The white belt is worn by a beginner. 3 The shin and instep pads are worn for protection when free sparring, and in competition. 4 The headguard, 5 foodpads and 6 hand-mitts must all be worn in tournaments. They are all padded with foam or sponge.

5

SUPER

Of the many martial arts that exist in Asia today, the Korean method of unarmed combat called taekwondo is perhaps the newest on the scene. It began life under its present name in 1955, although its roots stretch back nearly 2,000 years. The mother art was called 'hwarang do' or 'way of the flowering manhood'. During the Japanese occupation of Korea (1910–1945) Japanese influences were introduced into the existing Korean martial arts. The Koreans adapted many karate techniques and incorporated them into their training curriculum. At first sight, indeed, taekwondo and karate look very similar — that is until the Korean adepts of taekwondo unleash their awesome kicking power.

The headquarters of the World Taekwondo Federation are in a building called the Kukkiwon in Seoul, South Korea. It was there that in 1973 the first taekwondo world championships took place. As a result of the growing numbers of taekwondo practitioners, taekwondo has been listed as an Olympic sport and will be demonstrated at the 1988 Olympics. This achievement owes much to the work, since 1955, of the sport's modern 'father', General Choi Hong Hi.

THE THEORY OF TRAINING

Freely translated, taekwondo means 'hand and foot way'. It is a martial art which trains both the mind and the body and the student's attitude is of supreme importance, since many of the techniques, especially the exotic kicks, can be dangerous. It is essential to develop the 'right' attitude towards instructors and fellow students and to show respect for elders. Through self-discipline the student will learn to submerge his ego; ultimately he will not feel the need to prove his worth, either to himself or to others.

All instructions regarding techniques and all directions are given in the Korean language. The training place is called a 'dojang'. Before entering it, a student must make a formal bow at the doorway as a mark of respect.

THE FIRST STEPS

When a beginner joins a club the first thing he will become aware of is that great emphasis is placed upon training exercises and stretching, more so in taekwondo than in most other martial arts. Stretching exercises are especially important to enable students to perform the fantastic kicks that are the hallmark of taekwondo. Early training begins with simply punching and blocking, for both defensive and counter-attacking purposes. These are then linked together in a set logical sequence to teach the beginner continuity of movement.

■ Basic block 1: the starting position.

2 The attacker steps forward starting to punch, while the defender moves back starting to block.

3 The defender cocks her arms in the block position.

A new student is given the traditional uniform that all practitioners wear, called a 'tobok'. It consists of a loose shirt, or tunic, with baggy pants, tied together in the middle with a belt. The colour is white, to denote an absolute beginner. A student starts at tenth class, which is called 'kup' and works his way towards the level of proficiency of an instructor and his first dan, or black belt. This is an example of the striking similarities between karate and taekwondo. All students are informed by their instructor of the strict code of taekwondo. That stresses, above all, that one should defend first and attack second. A direct attack should never, outside of sporting purposes, be made against another person. Taekwondo exists to preserve life, not to take it.

To derive benefit from taekwondo training, the body has to be in peak physical condition. A student undergoes a prolonged period of performing stamina exer-

4 She completes the block with her outer forearm, in a walking stance.

5 The defender then lands a reverse punch.

■ Self defence 1: the starting position.

2 The attacker moves forward from a walking stance
to throw a front kick.

3 The defender moves back and places her arms in a
cocked position.

4 The attacker continues to release the kick.

5 The defender completes her outer forearm lower
section block against the front kick.

6 The attacker's kicking leg is swept to one side by
the block.

7 The defender is now in a position to counter-attack.

8 The defender lands a reverse punch to the middle section.

cises aimed at raising the heart rate and improving overall fitness. Exercises that accomplish this are swimming, short-term jogging (about half an hour a day) and skipping. These stamina exercises are supplemented by a programme of exercises set up by the instructor in the dojang. Apart from the standard exercises seen in most of the martial arts — sit-ups, press-ups and touching the toes — taekwondo training takes the beginner through a suppleness regimen designed to develop muscle strength and maximum flexibility.

(These flexibility exercises must always be preceded by warm-up exercises. The body should never be asked to stretch while it is still cold.)

The stretching exercises begin with the student sitting on the floor with his legs straight out in front of him and knees together. The upper body, or torso, falls forward, making sure that the bend originates from the lower back, not from the shoulders. The head is kept upright all the time. When the body is bent forward as far as it will go, the leg muscles are held tense and the position maintained for a count of ten. The body then relaxes. This procedure is repeated about five times. A follow-up to this exercise consists of grabbing hold of the balls of the feet with both hands, which increases the stretch. At first simply managing to grab the feet will prove to be an effort. But with practice the student will be able to lift his feet off the floor.

Another exercise is the open-leg stretch. The student sits on the floor and opens his legs in front of him, pushing his body weight forward as far as it will go. He then stretches out his arms and attempts to grab the sole of each foot. If at first this proves too difficult, an alternative method of grabbing the ankles may be substituted until the area becomes more stretched and flexible with use.

The next stretching exercise involves two people. The student lifts his leg into the air and places it on his partner's shoulder. The partner then pushes the leg further up into the air. The student performing the exercise can find his balance by resting his free hands somewhere on his partner's person. The legs should be gently stretched in this exercise. On no account should they be pushed straight up or in a jerky movement. The pressure should be even and there should be no excessive stretching. Once one leg has been exercised, the procedure is repeated with the other.

Rigorous stretching exercises and taekwondo go hand in hand, for without pushing the muscles beyond their normal use, the sinews and tendons will not gain the elasticity that is required for dynamic kicking techniques. The heart of taekwondo is to be able to deliver a kick, with power, to any target that is beyond the range of one's hands. But because many of the muscles are not stretched in ordinary daily activities, there is a great danger of spraining or tearing, especially at the beginner's stage. Great care should therefore be taken to stretch them gradually. All stretching exercises should be practised every day, not just at the weekly or twice-weekly training sessions at the club. It is important, once the stretching procedure gets underway, that the elasticity of the joints and muscles be maintained. The student should attempt to hold the stretched position of each exercise for as long as possible.

■ Hand conditioning: knuckle push-ups, taking care to keep the body straight.

■ A front leg-stretching exercise; from a walking stance throw up the leg, keeping the knee joint locked and toes pulled back into a high position.

■ Hamstring stretch 1: the foot is placed on the lowered shoulder of the partner.

2 Keeping the knee locked, the partner holds the outstretched hands and begins to stand upright.

3 The partner stands up straight, supporting the leg in a high position.

■ Turning kick exercise 1: stand on one leg and raise the knee into a hurdling position.

2 Pull the knee up to the highest position possible, while maintaining balance.

■ The front kick 1: begin by driving the hips forward.

2 Bring the knee up into a cocked position.

3 Deliver the kick to the target with the leg at full stretch, using the ball of the foot.

LEARNING THE KICKS

Three of the most important aspects of taekwondo kicking are these: (1) only use full power in the kick when the leg is fully extended; (2) when delivering a kick, raise the kicking knee and leg high and maintain a straight line through the body; and (3) give special attention to the hips and legs, which are the tools for ensuring explosive kicking power.

Almost all parts of the foot are utilized as weapons — the heel, the ball, the arch, the instep and the outside edge.

A beginner learns the same basic kicks in taekwondo as he would in karate. These are the front kick, the side kick, the back kick and the roundhouse kick. They are explained in the previous chapter. The kicking manoeuvres explained here are examples from the next level of instruction. They include kicks that can be delivered from any height (the spinning hook kick and the jumping front kick) and low spinning and sweeping kicks (the drop spin kick and the drop side kick). Taekwondo places great emphasis, of course, on flying kicks, and it is not unusual for two opponents to be in the air at the same time, one executing an attack and the other an airborne block or counter attack.

■ The high side kick 1: pull the knee up and forward, into a cocked position.

2 Deliver the kick while pivoting on the standing foot. Push the hips around fully into the kick, delivered with a footsword.

■ The spinning back kick 1: spin through 180°, drive backwards and out with the hips.

2 Deliver the kick to the target with a footsword.

■ The axe kick 1: begin to pull back the leg.

2 Raise the foot to the highest position possible.

3 Drop the kick straight down onto the opponent, using the heel of the foot.

■ The jumping front kick 1: drive upwards and forwards, thrusting the leg out to strike with the ball of the foot.

2 Maintain good balance on landing, with the hand in the guard position.

THE SPINNING HOOK KICK

This kick gains its effect from having the whole of the body weight behind it. The attacker faces his partner in a left fighting stance (this, again, is virtually the same as in karate) and shifts his body weight to the left leg. Then, turning clockwise, with the head turning first, followed a split second later by the body, he raises his back (right) foot, all the time glancing over his right shoulder to watch his opponent. As the right leg is lifted on the turn, it should remain high and close to the body. The attacker now completes the turn and thrusts his right leg out towards his opponent. At this stage, strength and power are not important. Speed is. Therefore use minimal strength to enhance speed and mobility. The foot is aimed at the face of the opponent and the kicking leg is bent at the knee in a snap motion down across the opponent's face.

THE JUMPING FRONT KICK

The jumping front kick is one of the most spectacular kicks in taekwondo. It is executed off the forward leading leg. The student begins with his right foot forward, with most of his weight resting on the left leg. In a kind of skipping movement he shifts his weight to the forward, leading right leg, scooping the left foot in front of the right knee and jumping off with the right leg so that it passes the left foot again. Led by the right hip, the right leg continues forward and thrusts to full extension at the opponent. As the kick strikes home, the entire right leg and the right side of the lower back are completely tensed. The power of the kick comes not from any knee snap, but from the line of tension which runs from the lower back the whole length of the right leg. A variation on this technique is the jumping front kick off the rear leg.

■ The jumping reverse turning kick 1: jump high, spinning through 180°.

2 Rotate the hips into the kick, to strike with the heel of the foot.

■ The jumping turning kick: strike with the ball of the foot, keeping the back leg tucked up.

■ Chung moo pattern 1: The rear foot stance is adopted with the hands ready for a twin knife block (left) which will be changed to a leading hand block during a 360°–jump (above) 2.

3 Coming down, changing the block, on completion of the jump and turn.

4 Landing in the rear foot stance with a knife hand block to the middle section.

5 Ready to move into the next stage of the pattern.

6 Starting position for chung moo pattern.

THE JUMPING SIDE KICK

Of all the kicks in taekwondo, the jumping side kick has probably received the most attention from the public, no doubt because its execution looks devastating and spectacular.

The student positions himself with the right foot forward, and the body weight evenly distributed. Using a slight pushing action, he shifts the weight on to the extended right leg while at the same time skipping with his left foot towards the extended right leg and almost simultaneously jumping off the ground with the right leg. In the split second that the student is airborne, both legs are cocked, with the right leg in readiness to kick outwards. At the peak of the jump the right leg lashes out horizontally towards the target. As the practitioner comes in to land, so to speak, the left, or guard, leg extends downwards ready to touch the floor. The right leg follows it and the student arrives back at his original stance. It is important, when executing this technique, that the right hand be held high, both to guard and to be ready to punch in the event of a counter-attack.

■ The sweep 1: The attacker throws a turning kick, while the defender drops down.

2 The defender begins to spin through 180°.

3 The defender sweeps the attacker's standing leg.

4 The attacker is swept to the ground with no defence.
5 The defender then cocks her knee ready for a turning kick.

THE DROP SPIN KICK

The student begins in the familiar free-fighting stance, with the left foot forward. Shifting most of the body weight to the right leg, he pivots clockwise in a 180-degree arc, taking care to keep a watchful eye on his opponent. He then suddenly drops to the ground on the left knee, placing the left hand on the floor in front of him. The left knee is then jerked forward while the right leg is extended in a clockwise arc. The instant the right leg goes out, the right hand is dropped to the floor so that the body is supported by both hands. Power is added to the sweep by tensing the lower buttocks and the right leg scythes along the floor, taking the opponent's feet from under him.

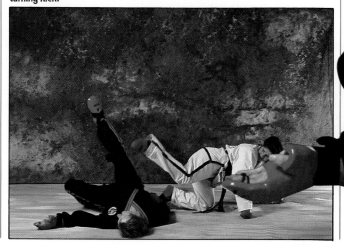

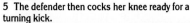

THE DROP SIDE KICK

This kick is especially useful when a fighter has been knocked to the ground and his opponent is closing in for the kill, although in training it is learned from a standing position. Placing the right leg forward, the student leans back over his left leg and drops his hands to the floor, while keeping watch on his opponent over the right shoulder. As the hands go down to the floor, the right knee is cocked up near the right shoulder. At this point the student should be supporting himself on his hands and the ball of his left foot. Now the right leg is thrust out with the foot travelling in a straight line towards the opponent. When the attacking leg is at full extension, the shoulders, the muscles in the right leg and the entire right side of the lower back and buttocks are completely tensed, and an incoming opponent, met by this sudden kick, shooting upwards from the ground, is immediately stopped dead in his tracks.

BEGINNING THE STANCES

Early basic training in taekwondo involves learning about the blocks, stances and strikes, using both the legs and the fists. Correct posture is vital to perform techniques

6 The defender drives home the turning kick to the head.

■ The reverse turning kick 1: the student begins to pivot through 180°.

2 He throws the hips into the kick.

3 He lands the kick with the heel of the foot.

properly. Leaning the body forward or to the side may result in a weakened balance, thus negating the effectiveness of the technique. It is therefore extremely important that the basic stances be thoroughly understood and properly practised.

The stability of a stance depends upon the distribution of the body weight. Lower stances, for instance, are more stable than taller ones, and, being solid and powerful, are naturally resistant to sudden attacks. On the other hand, what they gain in power they lose in speed and mobility. The taller stances, in which the practitioner adopts an almost upright position, are fast but weak. A strong attack by an opponent against a fighter in a tall stance can force him to back off, because the stance is too weak to stand its ground. The stance that is adopted therefore depends on circumstances. Each stance is capable of performing what is required of it in the right context. It is up to the practitioner to decide which stance is best suited to a particular purpose. It is a question of using the right tool for the right job.

Some stances may be held for only a fraction of a second, just long enough to provide the correct arrangement of balance, position and technique availability. In some stances the feet are flat on the floor; in others one or both feet may be raised at the heel. The time taken to flip from one stance to another must be fleeting. Nothing can be more devastating to a fighter than to be caught by his opponent midway between one stance and another.

In taekwondo the basic stances resemble those used in karate — the forward stance, which is achieved by extending the leading foot forwards, with the feet at shoulder width, and the back stance, which is formed by transferring the body weight to the back, supporting leg, with the hip lying above the bent, supporting knee. The back stance is especially effective for kicking, since the body weight can easily be shifted without changing position. The rear leg acts like a springboard, tensing the back foot outwards and facilitating a fast forward movement. The front, extended leg should be slightly bent. Caution must be taken never to straighten it, since to do so reduces the speed of front-leg kicks.

Probably one of the most popular stances in taekwondo is the 'walking stance', which is well suited to a number of conditions that require rapid movement in all directions. It gets its name from the fact that it requires a fighter simply to raise his hands in a defensive position and bend his legs slightly, almost as if he were walking down the street. A slight deviation from the walking stance quickly puts a student into the taekwondo fighting stance, in which the body is slightly inclined to present less of an open target and the fists are held high as in a boxer's pose.

■ Self defence 1: the attacker steps forward with a downward thrust.

2 The defender moves forward with a rising block.

3 She follows through with a palm heel strike.

4 She drives the attacker's head backward with the power of the strike.

5 The defender grasps the attacker's shoulders and raises her knee.

6 She drives a knee kick into the attacker's groin.

7 The defender pulls the attacker down and forward to immobilize him.

■ The walking stance should be one shoulder-width wide and one-and-a-half shoulder-widths long. Weight should be evenly distributed. The back leg is locked straight, with the back foot pointing forward and the front foot turned in slightly.

■ The sitting stance should be one-and-a-half shoulder-widths wide, with the feet kept straight. Weight should be evenly distributed.

The basic stances are called 'seogi'. Once the beginner masters the rudiments of these simple positions, he advances to body manoeuvring and turning, much of which concerns slipping from one stance into another. This is usually done by sliding, especially for covering short distances, whether in attack or defence. To slide forward from a forward stance, the student uses the forward thrust of the tensed rear leg to shift the front leg and body weight forward, the rear leg following naturally. To perform this sliding technique backwards, the student shifts the rear leg and body weight backwards, allowing the front leg to follow.

To cover a longer distance a technique known as double-stepping is employed. To double-step from a left forward stance, bring the rear foot slightly forward ahead of the body and then move the front foot forward to form a left forward stance once more. Keep the hips in the same direction throughout the manoeuvre. On no account should the legs be straightened.

To turn around from the forward stance to face in the opposite direction, adopt the standard forward stance, and then move the right foot about half a shoulder's width to the left, pivoting on the left foot and maintaining balance. Then turn to the opposite direction by stepping with the left foot about a shoulder's width to the left, thus ending up in a left forward stance in the opposite direction.

■ Basic block 1: the attacker begins to make a knife hand strike.

2 The defender places his arms in the correct position to execute a forearm block.

3 The attacker completes the strike, which is blocked.

4 The defender counters with a reverse punch to the floating ribs.

THE HAND TECHNIQUES

Because taekwondo was originally designed as an art of self-defence, blocking techniques are highly developed and refined. Taekwondo practitioners are not allowed to instigate an attack. Beginners are therefore instructed in the blocking capabilities of the art first, though in effect, of course, defensive movements also have an attacking function. A strong block can of itself inflict sufficient pain to deter an attacker.

The basic defence blocks are virtually identical to those used in karate. The forearm downward block, the inner forearm outward block and the rising block all have the same basic application as the blocks in karate, the only difference being that they are executed with much more force.

Taekwondo makes great use of evasion in its blocking and countering techniques. A slight body shift by the defender is undoubtedly the best form of defence against a strong punch from a much bigger and heavier opponent, though the defender should always have a backup block ready, in case the attack is only diverted, not completely sent off course. To meet force with force is successful only if the defender is as strong as the attacker. Since this is rarely so, a deft body evasion, backed up with a counter-block just before the moment of the attack's impact, almost always pays dividends. Correct body movement can reduce the force of an attack by 75 per cent.

A block should be used as a deflection, not as a head-on challenge to an oncoming technique. Sometimes an open-palm block can deflect a hard, solid punch much more easily than, say, a forearm block. The slapping action of the open palm is enough to make a punch miss its intended target. The knife block can also be used in a

Facing a knife attack 1: The defender prepares to meet the attack.

2 The attacker raises the knife ready to attack.

3 The defender moves forward to close the distance and block.

4 The defender blocks and prepares to strike.

chopping and thrusting motion. When a kick is employed by an attacker, the force behind it is very powerful and a head-on clash may well break the defender's arm. Various other methods of defence are, however, available to the taekwondo practitioner. One is the hammer fist block. This is a block that sweeps in a downward arc across the lower part of the body, connecting with the incoming kick near the ankle and knocking it out to the side. The practitioner utilizing this block steps up to meet the kick as it is coming in, thus meeting it before it has gained full momentum and power.

All the techniques in taekwondo are flexible and allow the practitioner to change his mind at the last minute as to which block or punch will provide him with the best defence or counter-attack. The downward hammer fist, for example, which can deflect a kick may also be instantly converted into a forearm scoop. This is an effective scooping block that curls under a kick aimed at the mid-section of the body and throws it to the side. If the defender gets enough of his own body weight behind the scooping block, the attacker's kick can be diverted off course and the attacker upended.

After learning the blocks, the beginner is introduced to striking techniques. The fist techniques of taekwondo in-

5 The defender strikes with the palm heel to the point of the chin.

6 She follows through with an elbow strike.

7 The defender slips an arm around the attacker's neck to form a head lock.

8 She pulls the attacker forward and drives the knee into the attacker's groin.

■ Straight fingertip thrust.

■ Back knuckle strike.

■ Reverse knife hand strike.

■ Inward knife hand strike.

■ Palm heel strike.

■ Basic punch.

■ Elbow strike: the point of the elbow makes contact.

■ Ridge hand strike.

■ The downward block 1: the block begins with the hands back to back, blocking arm on the inside.

2 The block moves downward and out; using the outer forearm, the other hand is pulled towards the hip.

■ The front leg hook kick 1: the attacker closes the distance.

2 She raises the knee into a cocked position.

3 The attacker lands the kick to the head, using the heel.

volve lunge punches, reverse punches, back fists and hammer fists — all of them similar to the basic karate punches described in the previous chapter. The hand techniques of taekwondo utilize focused power. It is a quite different power from that of the kicking techniques. Relaxation gives a punch an extension of an inch or so and therefore extra penetration towards the target. Every hand strike, whether clenched-fist or open-palm, must be relaxed until the moment of impact. This relaxation, combined with a turn of the hips to bring the shoulders into alignment, gives maximum power to the strike.

The power of the punch is concentrated in a small area of the knuckles. The arm is rotated just before impact, so that the fist hits the target in a type of screwing motion. Taekwondo practitioners build up the calluses on their knuckles by performing press-ups on them, although there is evidence that prolonged conditioning in this way causes metacarpal damage. Certainly calluses seem to enhance the fists' potential hitting power. The open palm is also an effective weapon, because the fingers are free to convert into finger jabs at the throat or eye gouges.

PUTTING IT ALL TOGETHER

The stage arrives when the beginner is ready to put all his basic techniques together. These combinations, as they are called, involve simple one-step punching and blocking techniques, but even of beginners a greater variety of kicks is expected, nor surprisingly in view of the emphasis that taekwondo places upon them. These combinations are used in controlled free sparring, which is termed 'kyoruki'. Free sparring accustoms beginners to being attacked and teaches them how to handle certain situations using the techniques they have been taught up to that stage. In kyoruki there is no set pattern of attacking and defending; the student uses his own judgement and applies the moves as necessary to block and counter-attack.

A combination is perhaps not quite so simple as the beginners first believe. Although it is a bringing together of basic techniques, certain movements in the kicks and punches must be altered slightly. Throughout the first months a beginner learns that in executing the basic reverse punch and the lunge punch, his hands have to withdraw back to the body in order to repeat the procedure over and over again. In sparring, this is not such a good idea, since the techniques do not lend themselves to repetitive actions. A certain amount of modification is desirable, which, while retaining the same amount of power and thrust, makes the movement fluid, not static.

Combination techniques comprise a host of different

■ The take-down and punch 1: the sparring partners take up positions.

2 The attacker throws a turning kick.

3 The defender moves forward and grasps the attacker's leg.

4 The defender sweeps the standing leg of the attacker.

5 The attacker falls to the ground with no defence.

6 The defender moves forward for the counter-attack.

7 The defender punches to the groin.

■ Changing the kick 1: the partners take up sparring positions.

2 As the attacker moves forward, the defender raises his leg into position for a side kick.

3 The defender switches to a turning kick to the head, catching the attacker as he moves forward.

moves, a kick and follow-up punch, for example, or a double-kick and then a punch. Combinations need not, of course, be made up entirely of attacking manoeuvres. They can include blocks with follow-up counter-attacks of kicking and punching. There is no end to the variety of patterns.

A typical attacking combination might be a side kick followed by a back kick. The attacker assumes a fighting stance, in this case a back stance, leading with the left leg and maintaining a left hand forearm guard. The attack begins with a side kick of the rear foot, which, when it has returned to the ground, is immediately followed by a back kick with the left foot. The back thrusting foot is then returned to the floor to form a right back stance with a forearm guarding block, which was the orginal position.

Combining a kick with a hand strike might happen as follows. Beginning in a left back stance, with the hand guard raised high, execute a roundhouse kick with the back foot to the side of the head. When the striking foot is back on the ground, the student falls automatically into a side-on right back stance. As the foot lands, deliver a left knife hand strike to the throat.

In a defensive combination, the student blocks first and then counter-attacks, as in the following sequence. The defender takes up a left fighting stance (all combinations are best practised from the fighting stance, as this allows a greater amount of protection and freedom of movement) and faces the attacker, who executes a front kick to the defender's mid-section. As the attacker's foot lifts from the ground, the defender is immediately warned that a kick is coming. Pre-empting the technique, the defender also raises his foot, which will be the right rear leg. The defender launches his pre-emptive counter-attack a split second after the attacker prepares to strike. Natural body movement does the rest. As the attacker's front kick sails in towards the target, the defender, by

launching an attack of his own, puts his body out of line of the oncoming kick. This is done as he lifts his rear leg to kick the attacker. The hips swivel around, presenting a side-on view to the attacker, who is by then too committed to his attack to alter the course of his kick without losing his balance. The defender's body, now side-on, is able to evade the attacker's front kick and strike home with his own front kick to his opponent's exposed groin.

A direct block in combinations may occur in the following way. A defender who is attacked by a front kick to the groin, blocks it with a downward palm strike. The attacker, sliding in closer, follows up with a punch to the face, which is once again blocked, this time with an outer block from a back stance. Having blocked two attacking techniques, the defender counters with a double punch to his opponent's face.

Many variations on the combination theme can be put into practice. When a beginner joins the competitive tournament circuit, he learns to forego many subtleties of the basic techniques in the interests of speed, strength being a less important quality in competitions. The basic lunge punch is dropped in favour of the short swift jab or the very fast reverse punch.

The kicking techniques employed on the tournament floor can vary tremendously. The preferred attacks are the circular kicking methods, which are not only very fast, but also difficult to block. As the beginner progresses to advanced techniques, he comes into contact with a very famous kicking method, called the axe kick. This spectacular technique uses gravity to enhance the force of the kick. From a forward fighting stance, the student swings his rear leg forward and upward until the knee comes to shoulder height. The leg is kept completely straight, with the hands held up close to the body as a rearguard defence. When the leg reaches the peak of the arc, the foot falls, heel first, toward the target area, which is

■ The inner forearm block 1: the arms are crossed, with the backs of the hands facing inward. The blocking arm is on the outside, defending the middle section.

2 The arms are pulled in opposite directions with equal force.

3 The blocking arm snaps across the body from right to left.

4 The block finishes in line with the shoulder, with the blocking arm at a 90°-angle, fist level with the shoulder.

■ Do San pattern movements 1: starting position.

2 Execute the outer forearm block, high to the side, in a walking stance.

3 Complete the block.

4 Continue with a middle section reverse punch.

■ Hwarang pattern movements 1: starting position.

2 A right hand punch, middle section, in the sitting stance.

3 A left hand palm heel block in the sitting stance.

4 A downward knife hand strike in the vertical stance.

usually the centre of the head or the collarbone. It is a devastating kick and one that is quite difficult to control once the foot has been set in its downward, attacking motion. It is often seen in competition, but for safety reasons the heel strike is substituted for the sole of the foot. Although this is a powerful technique, which can crack someone's skull open, exponents of it need to be aware that its very committed position makes them vulnerable to a sweeping counter-attack.

THE PATTERNS OF TAEKWONDO

Just as kung fu has its forms and karate its katas, so taekwondo has its version of set patterns. Taekwondo, unlike karate, stipulates that beginners must master all the basic techniques before attempting to practise the patterns. The pattern is a set series of combination techniques performed in a sequential order. The many, varied patterns take the beginner to advanced levels of the art, teaching him along the way a great mixture of different techniques containing all the essential elements of taekwondo. Because the pattern is a training aid, it allows the student to execute many of the dangerous kicking techniques in perfect safety, since he has no

■ The application of Do San 1: a wedging block used against a double-handed grab. Bring both hands up in front of the body together.

2 Break open the arms of the attacker using the outer forearms.

3 Deliver a front kick to the middle section.

4 Drive the attacker backwards with this kick to the stomach.

opponent. As in all the martial arts, the only avenue to perfection is the constant repetition of each pattern until the student can perform it without thinking — blindfolded and, in some schools, even backwards.

A pattern is designed to teach a beginner to perform movements in all directions of the compass. His imaginary opponent is visualized by the practitioner to be all around him. When practice first begins on the patterns, a beginner often loses direction instantly and executes a block or a kick to the wrong side. All instructors expect this, because the student has grown used to performing the basic techniques in a linear movement. Confusion occurs when the student is taken out of the 'rut', so to speak, and put in a situation where he has to execute flawless techniques from many different angles. This is why it is said that, to understand the taekwondo system, it is essential to understand the patterns. All the patterns begin and end at the same spot. The practitioner travels in all directions, executing various movements, with the final technique ending at the very point where he began.

The first pattern a beginner learns is called 'taegeuk', the correct name for which is actually 'taegeuk poomse'. 'Poomse' means 'pattern' and 'taegeuk' means 'the origin of all things in the universe'. This first pattern represents heaven and light and has 18 movements. It symbolizes the beginning, a taste of things to come. There are several varieties of the taegeuk, each forming a more advanced pattern than the one before. The patterns are a recent innovation, probably inspired by the Japanese kata, although the Korean governing body states that they originate from ancient Korean martial skills.

In the practice of patterns correct breathing is essential. For example, holding the breath during the execution of a move and then exhaling sharply at the moment of contact can concentrate power and increase speed. Deep breathing exercises, regularly practised, strengthen the diaphragm and help students to regulate their breathing during sparring. Breathing exercises should be performed at the end of each training session.

TAEKWONDO TRAINING WITH EQUIPMENT

Taekwondo practitioners use various aids to teach themselves correct timing in hand and foot techniques. One such aid is the punching ball, a leather bag with a rubber ball inside, which is fastened to the ceiling and floor with strong elasticated ropes. The centre of the ball should be at about shoulder height. Kicks, punches and elbow strikes can all be directed at the ball, and because it has a

■ Foot protector, top view.

■ Foot protector, bottom view.

■ Hand protector, back view.

■ Hand protector, inside view.

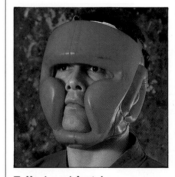

■ Head guard, front view.

■ Head guard, side view.

■ Taekwondo black belt: the gold bars distinguish rank.

■ Destruction techniques 1: preparing for a front elbow strike through three 1-in/ 2.5cm boards.

2 The striker pulls back and then follows through with the elbow strike, pushing the hips forward.

3 He maintains full power in the follow-through, not merely from the arm or shoulder, but from the whole body.

■ Destruction techniques 1: the knife hand strike. | 2 The striker concentrates his attention on the boards. | 3 A combination of speed and power.

certain amount of give in it, practitioners can get a more or less accurate feeling of how a punch or kick will feel against a human body. Several other kicking and punching bags are also used, including a large bag for developing power and a small kick bag for impact and timing. The bags are usually made of leather or canvas and hung from the ceiling on a rope or chain so that they may be easily raised or lowered. The base of the bag should rest at waist level. The bags are especially useful for practising flying kicks.

THE DESTRUCTION TECHNIQUES OF TAEKWONDO

Breaking bricks and wooden boards with the bare hands is part and parcel of martial arts training. Adepts at kung fu and karate use a number of techniques to smash through stacks of roofing tiles and concrete blocks with no apparent damage to their limbs. This is the showman side of those martial arts — displaying the ability to put mind over matter and accomplish the seemingly impossible with mere flesh and bone. Techniques of destruction, however, are much more central to taekwondo, which places great emphasis on them. Testing the efficiency of strikes, kicks and punches by directing them at bricks and tiles is a standard requirement for passing a grade and being promoted to the next level of proficiency. Long ago, the forerunner to taekwondo was a military skill, and taekwondo puts fighting theories into practice. The destruction tests are not simply a means for the practitioner to show off his power. They teach him the dynamic techniques of his art in order that he may be able to apply them, perhaps in a life-or-death predicament, on the streets. He has, therefore, to know in his own mind how much power he can harness into a technique and what he is capable of.

Nothing can be more daunting for a beginner than to

■ Side kick breaking 1: the striker raises the knee into a cocked position.

2 She thrusts out the leg, pushing the hips into the kick and using a footsword to break the boards.

step up and smash his fist or foot through a neatly arranged stack of wood or tiles, but that is only because his mind constructs a barrier. The hands and feet can be turned into deadly weapons capable of withstanding injury when they are applied to inanimate objects such as bricks and wooden boards so long as the practitioner approaches the matter with the right psychological outlook. Concentration is of the utmost importance. The student must gather all his energies, and with great stillness of mind, and the knowledge that he can push beyond ordinary human barriers, focus them on the point where the material at hand is to be broken.

Accuracy, speed and power are the prime elements in breaking techniques. Focusing the strike exactly on the point of impact is essential. If the strike is off-centre, the material will not break. Every object breaks once the limit

of its resilience has been passed. The student has to hone his skills to develop the power and speed to push the material past that limit. He must devote his whole mind to what he is doing. Nothing must be allowed to interfere. Penetration, focus, timing and mental confidence all play their parts in the achievement of a successful break.

Destruction training starts with practice on a special upright board, called the practice board. This hardens the parts of the body which are to be used to strike and break, each part that is to be hardened striking the board 40 or 50 times a day. For the first few days the hands and feet become too sore to practise with, but in time they become sufficiently conditioned to withstand the constant impact and calluses begin to develop in the key areas.

■ Destruction techniques 1: the spinning back kick. The striker pivots through 180°, spinning into the boards.

2 He lifts the knee while turning, thrusting the hips into the kick. The boards are broken with a footsword.

Students must pass through three stages of training before they are ready actually to break something. First, the hands and feet are toughened. Second, the speed to go through an object before it is hit out of the way must be developed. If the speed is not there, the student simply knocks the object over. Finally, the power of penetration to deliver a strike far beyond the object itself must be developed. When those techniques have been mastered, the student is ready to make his first serious destruction attempt.

■ The reverse turning kick 1: more speed is required for an air break because the boards are unsupported.

2 The striker smashes the boards with his heel.

3 He follows right through with the kick.

■ The knife hand break 1: the striker rises up to bring his full body weight to bear on the target.

2 He drops his body weight downward to strike right through the boards.

■ The forefist punch 1: the boards break under the power channelled through the front two knuckles.

2 The striker follows through until the arm is straight.

FREE SPARRING

When a certain degree of proficiency has been reached, a student takes part in free fighting with a partner. Although this precedes one-step sparring, caution must be exercised by fighters who are striking each other with hard techniques. Students who discover that free fighting is their forte usually become competition-orientated. But free fighting is only the first step on the road to real competition and, in order to instil confidence in students, it is performed according to set criteria. Free sparring, the next stage in training, is more demanding. The student has to figure out, through constant trial and error, what his best techniques are, which moves suit his weight, shape, size and build. The time spent on his daily training regimen must be increased. He has, indeed, come to the crossroads of his taekwondo career. If he is to continue, he should now be taking different movements and linking them together to form his fighting style — a format of defence and attack that becomes second nature to him. On his training bags, for example, he should be trying out various double and triple kicking techniques and working out a series of combinations, linked together with speed, timing, delivery, focus and his own personal footwork manoeuvres. Constant practice is the only means of forming his own stylized form of fighting.

A fighter must be versatile, able to exploit the full range of taekwondo fighting techniques. Therefore, although he trains in perfecting the moves that he does best, he should keep all the techniques polished. He must also be sharp-eyed, able to decide in a fraction of a second which technique to use in order to gain maximum advantage over an opponent.

At the outset of a free fight certain rules must be observed by the fighter. His stance should be relaxed, not fixed, since an unspecialized stance provides mobility and avoids the waste of valuable reaction time involved in switching to the best stance with which to meet an on-coming attack. As the two fighters move around the area looking for an opening in each other's defence, various manoeuvres to distract and break the opponent's concentration can be employed. The hands should be kept moving at all times, not held in a perfect, but rigid, high-guard defence. Standing off-set can present a smaller target area to the opponent and, by forcing him to strike at an alternative area, can trap him into leaving himself wide open.

In free fighting so many aspects come into play at the same time that newer students suddenly seem to be out of their depth. Yet all that is required is daily practice, interspersed with regular club training, and everything will become clear. Tactical understanding comes only

■ Free sparring 1: the attacker begins a reverse punch while the defender begins to spring.

2 The defender drives upward with a full knee spring out of the attacker's reach.

3 The defender delivers a jumping roundhouse kick to the head.

■ The side thrust kick 1: the attacker raises the knee to a high position, keeping the body upright.

2 He delivers the side thrust kick to the chin, pushing the hips into the kick.

through regular bouts of fighting, in which all the techniques used are directed toward the scoring of maximum points.

In actual competition, taekwondo exponents have to wear a specific, padded body armour, which is a sleeveless jacket fastened at the back with cord ties. Forearm and shin guards must also be worn in accordance with the strict safety standards laid down by the governing body. The groin guard is optional. Fights usually consist of three three-minute rounds, with a one-minute break between each round. In the individual fighting categories there are ten weight divisions for men and eight for women. The combatants try to score the most points possible, using techniques which involve actual body contact. The strikes and kicks, although not delivered with maximum power, as speed is more important, do land on the body with a certain amount of force. Knockouts are not uncommon at taekwondo tournaments. Points are awarded for skilfully delivered techniques, the kicks scoring more points. Because taekwondo is a combat sport, in which full-power attacks are allowed to the face and body, tournament contestants have to be of black-belt standard, but even so, many of the more dangerous techniques of the art are not permitted.

Having fought in club free sparring sessions and inter-club competitions, the student's energies and training skills will be directed towards gaining the coveted black belt of an instructor. Taking any test requires commitment; the black belt test takes the most commitment of all. The practitioner will have to train two or three hours a day, every day, week in and week out.

■ The reverse punch 1: the attacker moves forward for a back fist strike.

2 The defender drops low and counters with a reverse punch.

3 The defender side-steps the attacker after delivering the punch.

CHAPTER FOUR

NINJUTSU

NINJUTSU EQUIPMENT

1 The split-toed boots are called tabi. 2 The Ninja costume and face mask were black, for camouflage during night attacks; in the winter a white suit was worn to blend in with the snows of the mountains. 3 The chain is called a manrikigusari, which translates roughly as '10,000-power chain'; it was used for strangulation techniques. 4 The Ninja sword blade is shorter and straighter than that of the Samurai sword. 5 The throwing stars (shuriken) were usually concealed in an inside pouch of the Ninja costume, in multiples of seven; the number had a spiritual significance, denoting power. The sharp tips were usually coated in poison. 6 The Ninja claws were used for climbing, one pair strapped to the hands and another pair to the inside of the lower leg; the hand claws were also effective in trapping the sword blade of the Samurai warrior as he struck.

■ Preparation for wrist exercises 1: suppleness in the wrists is important.

2 Pull the hands down in front of the body, with the palms pressed together to stretch the wrist joints.

3 Extend the hands in front of the body and pull them back in toward the sternum.

THE ORIGINS OF THE NINJA

■ Ninjutsu began more than 800 years ago among the ninja people who lived in Japan. Japan was a society that was ruled by a warrior class, the samurai who controlled everything, the land, and its people. They were answerable only to their lord, the shogun. The ordinary peasant served the warrior's every whim. If a samurai wanted to kill a peasant, it was his right to do so. A peasant could never strike a samurai; if he did, it would mean his life. The ninja would not serve the samurai, and fled to the barren, cold, mountainous regions of Iga and Koga. There they trained in the arts of war. It is said that their art is based upon a great Chinese military text written by a general named Sun Tzu, *The Art of War*. Over the centuries the ninja (the word means 'stealers–in') trained from the cradle to the grave in every known martial art. Their forte was espionage and assassination, by any means possible. But their training also taught them to reach spiritual heights, by pushing their bodies and minds to limits far beyond that of normal human endurance. In a way, they became the peasants' warrior class.

Training for a ninja began almost as soon as he could walk. Childhood games were designed to inculcate expertise in unarmed combat, swordwork, weaponry, camouflage, escape and evasion. In time, the ninja warriors came to be feared throughout Japan. Even the mighty samurai looked over his shoulder if a ninja was known to be operating in his area. The ninja learned to fight to survive; for if he failed, death would surely follow.

Over the centuries, while ninjutsu was being practised in secrecy, no one knew anything about the art except the ninjas themselves. When Japan emerged into the modern era, and feudalism collapsed, however, the ninja were absorbed into Japan's secret service and special services groups. And when the martial arts boom came to the West in the early 1970s, adventurous practitioners began searching for something a little different. Two such men, an Israeli named Doron Navon and an American, Stephen Hayes, found a ninjutsu headmaster living in Japan who came from an unbroken line of ninja instructors dating back almost 800 years. It was these two men whose diligent study of this ancient art brought it, within the last ten years or so, to the attention of the Western world.

THE SEARCH FOR INSTRUCTION

Because ninjutsu is relatively new in the West, instructors are a bit thin on the ground. All ninjutsu practised in the world today comes under the banner of Dr Masaaki

■ Clasp the hands behind the back to stretch the shoulder joints and back muscles.

■ The entangled arm exercise, which stretches the fingers.

■ With the thumb on the back of the hand, fingers gripping the wrist, bend the wrist inwards and twist it away.

忍
術

Hatsumi and his Bujinkan dojo group in Japan. In the West, the society responsible for the teaching of the warrior traditions, as they are known, is called 'The Shadows of Iga', which is responsible for the training and licensing of ninjutsu instructors under the direct authority of the grandmaster in Japan.

Once a beginner finds a ninja group (it is always called a group, not a club), he is interviewed by the instructor about why he wants to learn the art. If the instructor is satisfied by the reasons, the new student is formally introduced to the rest of the class, which is always called the 'family'. All ninja training has one primary objective — to free the practitioner from a rigid training structure. It is believed that following a set course limits the student and eventually strangles him in technique for technique's sake. The aim is, through technique, to achieve total freedom of self-expression. This theory is quite the opposite from that underlying the conventional martial arts' training methods. Kung fu, karate and taekwondo all rest on a firm foundation of basic techniques that serve as the building blocks which every practitioner must use if he wishes to become an adept. Ninjutsu is somewhat different. Although it does have basics to guide students through the rudiments of movements and techniques, they are only there as 'starters', so to speak, not as integral parts of the art. Each new student grasps these bare fundamentals chiefly in order to acquaint himself with a martial art. For many people ninjutsu eventually becomes a way of life.

A new student starts by learning how to use his body to the best advantage, not just parts of the body, like the arms or legs, but all of it. He undergoes a period of physical conditioning, or body flexibility training, called 'junan taiso'. This training teaches him how to become supple. The ninja rely purely upon natural body movement for effective self-defence. Their exercise regimen is designed to relax the muscles, not wear them out through prolonged conditioning.

A typical training exercise might begin with the student lying on his back, with his hands clasped behind his head and his legs extended. Twisting the body from this position, he then brings the right elbow down to meet the rising left knee, without unclasping the hands. He then lies down on the ground again. Next, the left elbow comes down to meet the slightly raised right knee. The whole procedure is repeated about 10 times. A single breath is released throughout the exercise, inhaling taking place again only when the body has returned to the ground. This exercise strengthens the lower torso and the waist.

An upper torso exercise might begin with the student raising his right arm over his right shoulder, while moving his left arm around his back and upwards to meet the right one. When the two hands meet, he clasps them together, then twists and bends his body as much as possible without letting the hands release their grip. After a few moments the hands are switched to the opposite direction and the procedure is repeated.

■ Side bending exercise to stretch the upper body 1: first to the left, with the right arm held aloft.

2 Hold the left arm aloft.

3 Repeat the stretching exercise to the right.

TAIJUTSU

Taijutsu is the art of using the body in ninjutsu and was once the Japanese warrior's method of unarmed combat. It was absorbed into the ninjutsu system because its fighting principle is the necessity to be proficient in every possible situation, defensive or offensive. No distinctions are made according to whether the attacker is heavier or lighter, smaller or larger, or weaker or stronger. The system had to work in all cases for the ninja to survive. Taijutsu is thus an all-round method for using the body's natural movement to avoid being hit, while at the same time preparing the defender to counter-attack. It has many branches, including grappling, throwing, locking and bone-breaking, rolling and breakfalls, plus strikes aimed at muscle destruction. A student trains in every branch of the art in order to arrive at a spontaneous fighting mode capable of defending him in any situation.

Ninjutsu has no set stances, the reason being that a stance implies a static nature, and during an attack roots the defender to a spot, even if only for a moment. Ninjutsu discourages rigid poses and encourages intricate footwork. A type of stance is used by beginners, but only as a starting-point, to be abandoned later.

Taijutsu rests on a concept of body familiarity that takes the practitioner beyond what he perhaps thought was possible. When attacked, a practitioner can place himself out of harm's way simply by shifting his feet from one area to another or transferring his body weight from one foot to another. And without adopting a static pose,

he remains in a position to retaliate. Since the art of ninjutsu began, set stances have never been used. Subtle shifts in body weight and foot positioning seem to neutralize all kinds of attacks. The defender appears to envelop the attacker without exerting himself in any way. As an old Chinese saying puts it, 'deviate an inch, and lose a thousand miles'. In other words averting a strike by an inch is as good as averting it by a mile. Ninjutsu practitioners scorn the excessive energy and movement which the other martial arts put into a block or evasion.

In ninjutsu every confrontation is unique; methods of counter-offensive strikes cannot be worked out beforehand. Yet because the beginner needs a springboard from which to develop his techniques, instructors teach a series of basic positions. These positions are not stances, but merely starting-points from which to launch either an attacking or a defensive movement. There are four main positions — unarmed natural, defensive, attacking and receiving — plus two others, the 'bear' and the 'crane' positions.

When under attack, the ninja student, instead of blocking and counter-punching as the fist comes towards his face, moves his body at an angle, thus putting it out of harm's way. He then instantly strikes the inside forearm of the attacker's punching arm, not only stopping the punch from being redirected, but destroying the muscles and rendering the arm useless for a further attack.

Ninjutsu teaches students not to block, but directly to counter-attack the opponent's attacking limb. This absence of standard defensive moves in response to an attack is one of the unique aspects of ninjutsu. The de-

■ Stretching the lower back 1: extend the legs so that both feet touch the floor behind the head. Support the back with the hands.

2 Return the legs to the bent position.

3 Extend the legs with the toes pointing upwards.

4 Return the legs to the front sitting position and reach forward to grip the feet.

5 Bend forward, pulling downwards, keeping the back straight.

■ The front rolling technique 1: with the knees bent and legs apart stretch towards the floor.

fensive attack of the ninja student causes more damage to the attacker than a block would. For one thing, the sudden, intense pain which it inflicts unsettles the opponent's mind, and during this period of uncertainty the ninja is at liberty to press home his retaliatory manoeuvre.

Suppose an attacker strikes with a punch to the face. The ninja student merely leans (or slides) backwards, pushing his back leg further back to take the supporting weight of his body. The front leg follows very quickly. Thus he retreats out of harm's way, though not so far as to be out of reach. The opponent's fist, fully extended, is irretrievably exposed and the ninja, in a see-saw movement of the body, rocks forward into full fighting range and strikes it on the back of the hand just below the wrist. His knuckles smash into the soft, fleshy parts of his opponent's hand, causing all the more pain because the attacker's fist is tensed. In an instant the striking fist is rendered useless, though little effort has been required of the ninja. The natural movement of his body has done virtually all the work.

From the very beginning a ninja student is guided by his instructor to think for himself. Once he becomes familiar with his body movements and understands the importance of reacting naturally, rather than following a strict code of responses and counter-attacks, he finds that he is able to move much more freely. The unconventional ninja movements enable him to flow naturally from one position to another and thus continually change his angles of attack. He can counter on both horizontal and vertical planes by slipping under, over or even beyond his assailant's attacks. By constantly changing his angles of attack he is able, although only momentarily, to disappear from his attacker's line of sight, thereby making it easier for him to retaliate effectively and escape.

2 Shift the weight forward onto the front leg and tuck the head in, to initiate the rolling motion.

3 Continue to roll forward, keeping the body compact.

▐ NINJA ROLLING TECHNIQUES ▐

Ninjutsu is made up of many skills. Each has a part to play in enabling the student to cover all aspects of a fighting confrontation, to arrive at what ninjutsu calls the 'winning edge' over his opponent. Unlike most other martial arts, ninjutsu allows its instructors great freedom to teach the art as each of them sees fit. Even so, at the beginning stages a common theme is followed, founded on the basic aspects of the art.

The martial art of jiu jitsu employs many methods of falling correctly, each devised to enable a practitioner to execute a particular throw. Ninjutsu also has a whole range of falling, rolling and tumbling techniques, but for a different end altogether. During the execution of a roll a

4 Allow the forward motion to take you out of the roll and into a standing or kneeling posture.

■ Shizen no kamae (natural posture) 1: facing the attacking swordsman.

2 The defender instantly shifts his body weight in preparation for the roll.

3 He rolls away as the swordsman strikes downward.

4 The defender continues to roll until he is out of the danger area.

ninja seeks to merge himself with the terrain, to achieve a kind of unity between his body and the rolling surface. Outdoors, for instance, this is done by lowering the body mass close to the ground, thereby allowing the legs to direct the body in the direction of the movement.

When a student performs any type of roll, his entire body should work as a unit, every limb contributing to the smooth execution of the roll. In the basic side roll, for example, the body moves to a position leaning in the direction of movement, the head and the arms taking the lead, followed next by the hips and then by the legs. Ninja rolling techniques are an effective way to close distances; moreover, they reduce the body mass, thus making the practitioner a smaller target.

Rolling is one of the first skills a beginner practices. At first he may be wary of injuring himself, but with prolonged practice the manoeuvres become second nature to him and at any given moment he can launch himself

into a forward or backward roll, or even from side to side. Rolling also has its psychological aspects. For the ninja to be able to execute his rolling skills on concrete flooring as well as he can on soft earth he needs to be free of any psychological hang-up. Otherwise, if he were attacked on the street, his concentration would slip for a moment as he paused to consider whether he would hurt himself if he were to throw his body into a roll on a concrete surface. The teacher therefore shows the student how to curl, or in some cases arch, his body in order to perform a roll on concrete or a solid tiled floor without his bones crunching against the surface and without pain. Pain, after all, can also be a great distraction in a life-or-death situation.

At all times during the learning of rolling procedures the instructor continually points out that a roll must feel good to the person doing it. It must become an automatic extension of his movement, as easy and as natural

忍術

■ Continuous shifting of position 1: the defender moves back as the punch is thrown; his left hand moves up to strike the underside of the attacker's forearm.

2 The defender begins to shift his weight backwards as the attacker attempts a second punch, and strikes at the underside of the forearm with the fist.

3 The underside of the forearm is struck again as the attacker continues to punch.

4 The defender drops toward the floor as the attacker steps forward to punch for the third time.

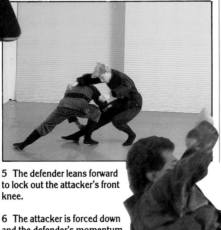

5 The defender leans forward to lock out the attacker's front knee.

6 The attacker is forced down and the defender's momentum takes him through into a front roll.

7 In one continuous movement, he completes the roll and strikes the attacker's head.

■ The shoulder lock 1: as the attacker grips, the defender draws him forward.

2 The defender then steps forward, bending the attacker's gripping arm, unbalancing him.

3 The defender continues to move forward, entangling his opponent's arm in order to come in close.

4 The defender completes a tight shoulder lock, with the palms placed together.

5 The defender begins to shift his weight downwards onto the leg of the attacker.

6 From a kneeling position, the defender throws his opponent to the floor.

as walking down the street. Once that is achieved, concentration is devoted to performing the rolls with maximum speed and minimum noise. After all, stealth is at the heart of all ninja techniques. One training device is to lay newspapers on the floor and then require students to execute forward and backward rolls on the paper without tearing it. A very common fault that beginners make on the forward roll is to slam the backs of the heels against the floor, which creates noise and can cause slight pain.

A correctly executed roll should involve no sliding contact between body and ground at any point. The ninja should imagine himself to be a ball rolling along the floor. When the movement is completed he should come out of the roll straight into a fighting stance, known as a 'kamae'. As he perfects his rolling manoeuvres, the student comes to understand that rolls not only provide a means to escape, from a throw, joint lock or strike, but also a method of covering ground that can be used as an offensive attack. The ninja must have at his command a sum total of fighting capabilities; he must be as much at home lying on the floor as standing upright on both feet.

Because of his ground-fighting ability, a ninja in the sitting combat mode is incapable of being thrown by the practitioner of another martial art such as judo, akido or even wrestling. By the very fact that he can launch an attack from a sitting position, he virtually nullifies most of their techniques. In a floor-fighting position, of course, the ninja sacrifices some mobility, but he gains the advantage, when fighting defensively, of being able to tackle an opponent bigger and stronger than himself. Altering the fighting arena by dropping to the floor enables a nine-stone ninja to overcome a fourteen-stone opponent. The bigger man is forced to strain downwards with his attack and commonly resorts to a foolish or reckless tactic to which he commits the whole of his attacking energy. The ninja is thus able to direct the attack off course and then strike with his own counter-attack — either a back thrust kick from the ground or a scything leg bar sweep to knock his adversary completely off balance.

The ninja believes that each fighting confrontation is unique. He therefore wastes little time on practising set manoeuvres. Martial arts clubs too often arrange simulated fights, the experience of which is of little value in a

■ Throwing technique 1: the attacker places his right arm under his opponent's left arm and raises it to the opponent's shoulder, in order to unbalance him.

2 The attacker turns, trapping the defender's arm.

2 He steps across his opponent and drops his weight downward.

4 The attacker rotates forward from the waist to throw his opponent.

5 He completes the throw.

6 After successfully completing any technique, the ninja is taught to maintain concentration and be ready for any counter-attack.

■ Defence against sword attack 1: the defender avoids the sword thrust by leaping sideways.

2 He strikes the back of the sword hand with the knuckles.

3 Maintaining his momentum, the defender moves towards the attacker, trapping both hands.

4 The defender raises his arms and twists the swordsman's arms upwards and to the side.

5 He steps behind the swordsman's right leg in preparation for the throw.

6 The swordsman is thrown to the floor.
7 The defender continues to twist the swordsman's wrist, while applying knee pressure to the elbow, to release the sword.

real fight. By judging a situation when it arises the ninja expert knows instantly whether to fall naturally into an attacking or defensive mode; and should the first movement fail, split-second timing, incorporating a myriad of twisting and spiralling body movements, can put him into a second defensive or offensive position without losing ground or yielding the advantage to his attacker.

The ninja's art of ground-fighting is a complete and comprehensive one and exists independently of the more commonly known jiu jitsu and judo. Although strictly speaking ground work is essentially a defensive system, it is versatile enough for the ninja adept to regain a lost advantage even against a larger and heavier opponent. Furthermore, because of its built-in element of surprise, it can have an absolutely demoralizing effect upon an assailant. It is these capabilities that lead other martial artists to call ninjutsu, quite erroneously, 'the art of dirty tricks'. The ninja, affectionately, calls it 'the art of winning'.

NINJA FIGHTING TACTICS AND WEAPONS

Fear of the dark is innate in man. It is the fear of the unknown, of what cannot be seen. Traditionally the ninja used the darkness as his ally. It became his cloak of invisibility, a mask enabling him to perform his covert activities. By developing their senses to overcome the psychological fear of the darkness at a very early age, in infancy in fact, the ninja people built up confidence in their ability to overcome even the unknown. The ninja could then go about under shield of darkness plying his deadly trade.

In modern ninja training, beginners are introduced to night-time training, performing all the disciplines normally practised in daylight hours. The purpose is to develop the senses other than sight. Listening for sounds, being aware of body movement and exploiting the sense of touch will heighten the ninja's general awareness of his everyday surroundings. Attacked in the daytime or at night, he is less likely to be taken by surprise. Because of the impracticalities of training constantly at night, ninja students usually train blindfolded instead.

Ninjutsu, again unlike most other martial arts, teaches students the use of certain weapons at a very early stage. Training is geared towards familiarity with various weapon groups rather than a set series of techniques. In this way the student is not limited to one or two specific weapons, but is able to pick up anything that will serve as a weapon and use it effectively. One of the most common implements that can be used as a weapon is a

■ Variation on sword defence 1: as the swordsman raises the weapon above his head, the defender uses his leading hand to check the downward cut and strikes to the ribs, using the thumb.

2 He lands a right heel kick to the inside of the swordsman's forward knee.

■ Deflecting the strike 1: a kick to the inside of the opponent's punching arm with the near leg.

2 The leg is pulled back into a guard position, in readiness for a second strike.

garden tool. It is this ability to convert everyday objects into weapons that gives the ninja student his fighting edge.

In a blade-fighting situation, a typical response to a sword thrust would begin with the student assuming a defensive posture. As the attacker lunges and his blade is in motion on a focused path, the defender can slip to the left or right and avoid the attacker's cut while at the same time turning the cutting edge of his own weapon towards the lunging attacker. The attacker, having missed his intended target, would then cut his own wrist or arm on the defender's sword. The ninja defender simply holds his position without having to do a thing or exert any unnecessary energy. The attacker's own momentum carries him automatically forward to the defender's blade.

stick. Traditionally the ninja trained with a short stick about three feet in length, called a 'hanbo'. 'Han' in Japanese means 'half' and a bo was a six-foot staff.

The hanbo is still used in modern ninja training. Training begins with learning how to grip the weapon across the palm so that it forms an extension of the arm when the wrist is held in a natural position. This diagonal, cross-palm grip is the fundamental method of holding all weapons for use in self-protection. It allows for total freedom of use without special body movements having to be learned. Strikes can be made in nine directions with little difficulty, by lunging and by striking horizontally, vertically or diagonally. By incorporating efficient foot movements into an attack with the hanbo, the body mass in motion, not the limb alone, drives the weapon to its target.

Sparring sessions are arranged in which two students face each other and make alternate strikes with the hanbo. One acts as a defender, the other as an attacker. At first, though some realistic aspects are introduced, this training simulates attacks and defences, because seeing something over and over again eventually takes away its shock value and it becomes commonplace.

Students of ninjutsu learn sword skills, or blade techniques, from very early stages in their training. The art of the ninja blade skills is termed 'ken-po'. It teaches practical skills in the handling of a sword and also incorporates daggers of various shapes and sizes. The formal training consists of fast-draw techniques for pulling a sword or knife from its scabbard and cutting with it in one simultaneous movement. Fencing skills are also taught, so that adepts can use the hand-held blade against an attacker's weapon, as are throwing skills (for hitting distant targets with the blade). Although the two-handed Japanese sword is used for some practice sessions, today's students of ninjutsu could use any kind of

■ Hoko no-kame (bear posture) 1: as the attacker punches, the defender drops his hand down from the forward defensive position.

2 The defender steps back to evade the blow and drops his weight downward.

3 He strikes to the underside of the attacker's punching arm.

4 The defender drops back again to repeat the technique.

5 Hoko no-kame: as the opponent initiates the third punch, the defender raises his hands into the hoko no-kame position and kicks the punch with the heel of the foot, back into the opponent's chest.

blade, whether a hunting knife, or even a kitchen knife.

Another bladed weapon used in ninja training is the famed throwing star, known as a 'shuriken'. Although television and films have made this star the symbol of the ninja, it is actually a multi-shaped weapon which comes in various sizes and styles. Sometimes it takes the shape of a short-bladed iron dart; sometimes it is shaped like the disc of a flying saucer, with a razor sharp edge. One of the early classical shapes, was that of an inverted swastika, which in ancient times was a sanskrit symbol of good luck. These razor-sharp, pointed throwing implements were usually kept in bunches of seven in a secret pocket of the ninja's black uniform. The shuriken does not have much accuracy at great distances. In the old days they were tipped with a fast-acting poison. When a ninja infiltrator was discovered in some castle grounds, he could effect his escape by hurling one or more of them at his pursuing enemy. Even if they did not kill the advancing enemy outright, once his skin had been punctured by the deadly tip, death would certainly follow.

Although these weapons are today considered archaic, ninjutsu students are expected to perfect some skills in several of them, because training with old weapons helps students to learn to improvise self-defence tools from everyday articles. To the ninja student no weapon can be obsolete, because any object may be used as a weapon.

Ninjutsu training encompasses eight methods of combat fighting: (1) taijutsu — the unarmed fighting method; (2) hichojutsu — leaping and climbing methods; (3) bojutsu — stick and staff fighting; (4) kenjutsu — blade fighting and throwing; (5) kusarijutsu — chain and cord weapons; (6) goton-po — the use of natural elements; (7) omshinjutsu — the art of disguise and invisibility; (8) heiho — military tactics.

But whatever branch of the art is being practised, the principles remain constant — agile footwork, power and speed are essential whether one is working with kicks, stick-fighting or blade techniques. The ninja fighting style is a series of flowing, simple moves, not a system of elaborate and complex techniques. Once the student has digested the fundamentals of fighting movements, he trains his mind to analyze how best to apply them. The advanced student undertakes meditation to improve the clarity of his mind and to learn how to relax totally. This enables him to make reflective observations during a combat situation, being in a 'receiving state'. When in the receiving state he can apply the unique offensive blocking method characteristic of the ninja fighting system.

As a means of practical development, the ninja student must practise meditation while sparring or training in techniques. The essence of ninjutsu is simplicity. The more elaborate a fighting style, the harder it is to master.

■ Unbalancing the attacker 1: as the attacker grips and punches, the defender strikes the punching arm.

2 The defender moves towards the attacker and grips the skin of his upper arm in order to unbalance him.

3 He steps across the attacker in one continuous movement and throws him to the floor.

The ninja system of fighting was developed by men of combat and to this day it retains the feeling of reality. In realistic defensive situations the student can rely on the directness and accuracy of his techniques to pull him through. All techniques in ninjutsu, although relatively simple, are highly effective.

Students of almost every martial art are encouraged to develop spiritual awareness. In the art of the ninja the development of the five senses is refined to an extent that almost borders on the mystical. Right from the first day the ninja student seeks to achieve harmony with his surroundings. The ninja philosophy teaches that this awareness comes from a mystical knowledge of the universe, such as was taught centuries ago by the Yamabushi mountain priests and refined and developed for use in combat. There is nothing exceptional in this teaching, which rests on the simple belief that by observing nature with an open and inquiring mind, a man may come to understand his relationship to the world and thereby to understand himself.

Ninja training of the mind includes 'kuji-kuri', or the art of finger-weaving. The practitioner clasps his hands together, holds them out in front of him and entwines his fingers into an intricate design. This is said to channel his mental energies towards the task at hand or a difficulty to be surmounted. By doing this finger-knitting the ninja student creates a certain mood within himself. There are five moods, or attitudes as they are called, in ninjutsu. They are named earth, water, fire, wind and void. Each state of mind serves as the foundation for a specific series of techniques.

In the earth attitude a student holds his ground solidly,

■ Defence against a kick 1: avoiding the attack and unbalancing the attacker.

2 The defender shifts his body weight to avoid the kick.

3 The defender moves towards the attacker in order to trap the supporting leg.
4 Shifting his weight forward, he collapses the attacker's supporting leg with pressure from the knee.
5 As the attacker falls forward, the defender continues to exert knee pressure downwards on the back of the leg.

■ Jumonji (crossed hand position) 1: The defender drops back and strikes the underside of the punching arm.

■ Boshiken (thumb strike): the defender shifts his weight forward to strike the attacker's ribs.

taking the attacker's onslaught without letting it affect him, as he knows that his strength will prevail. The adversary feels as though he is fighting against a rock which is impervious to everything he does.

In the water attitude a student shifts and flows, using distancing and unexpected movement to defeat his adversary. He aims to outfox his foe by his flexibility, and his adversary feels as though he is fighting against ocean waves that recede from his advances, then suddenly crash back on him again.

The fire attitude inspires a student to pursue his attacker with fierce intention. The harder the attacker fights back, the more intense the ninja's blows become. He is committed to injuring the opponent in direct proportion to the strength used against him, so that the harder the adversary fights, the more he is overcome by the dynamic response of the ninja. It is as though the attacker were fighting a forest fire; the more he attempts to beat it out, the more it engulfs him.

In the attitude of the wind a student fights with purely defensive moves, protecting himself without causing undue injury to the attacker. The student uses just enough force to discourage his adversary, who is meant to feel as though he is fighting a losing battle against the wind.

The void attitude imbues the ninja with a feeling of emptiness. He uses his creative powers in words and actions to create an environment in which there is no need to fight.

Through the teachings of this so-called mystical side of the art the student comes to realize that on many occasions attacks or confrontations do not come about by chance. They are the results of predicaments in which

3 The defender raises his hand, with the fingers extended in front of the attacker's eyes, to discourage forward movement.

4 The defender drops back again, before striking the opponent's left punching arm.

5 The defender lunges forwards, this time with a right-handed thumb strike to the ribs.

■ Yoko-o-aruki (cross-step) 1: the defender slips to the side, using the cross-step to evade the punch.

2 He continues to move away from the attacker.

3 He strikes at the outside of the attacker's punching arm.

4 He kicks to the attacker's left hip with a stamping action.

5 The defender, having floored his opponent, maintains his distance.

■ Sanshim tan ken (three-fingered strike)
1: the defender steps back to evade the punch.

2 The defender then begins to step forward to gather momentum for a counter-attack.

3 Sanshim tan ken: he strikes the opponent's solar plexus, using the full weight of the body.

■ The defender avoids the kick 1 by employing a cross step.

2 Keri keohi: the defender kicks against the underside of the attacker's kicking leg.

3 The technique spins the opponent off balance.

he has placed himself. The way that he reacts to situations, the way he thinks, can produce conflict. Therefore he learns to control events around him as much as possible and so avoid confrontations.

Ninjutsu teaches that all training is to be enjoyed, to be conducted in a happy atmosphere. The earnestness of the karate dojo is to be avoided; all techniques are practised in a lighthearted manner, though with purposeful intent. The ninja philosophy is that training does not have to be grim or painful to be effective. If a student's mind and body are used to being relaxed and natural and accustomed to responding spontaneously to various training situations, then he will be less likely to tighten up, become angry or scared, or lose control should a threatening situation arise in real life. Naturalness, being in tune with oneself, is the key. No matter what he runs into — a physical or emotional attack or an intellectual confrontation — the ninja student seeks to deal with it calmly. The art of ninjutsu is to live life in the way that one wants to live it.

One aspect of ninjutsu that a student has to learn is the special method of moving stealthily and unseen. Ten techniques, or styles, evolved down the centuries, exist for this purpose: (1) nuki-ashi — stealthy step; (2) suri-ashi — rub step; (3) shime-ashi — tight step; (4) tobi-ashi — flying step; (5) kata-ashi — one step; (6) o-ashi — big step; (7) ko-ashi — little step; (8) talaizami-ashi — small step; (9) wari-ashi — proper step; (10) tsune-ashi — normal step.

Another common stealth movement used by the ninja in former times was 'yoko-aruki', or side-walking. By moving the legs sideways, in a cross-step fashion, the ninja confused the enemy. To learn how to step carefully and in silence ninja youth were required to walk through

忍術

■ Oniku daki (demon crush) 1: the attacker grasps the defender's jacket, who in turn traps the gripping hand.

2 The defender moves back to over-extend and off-balance the attacker. He places his hand inside the attacker's grip.

3 Turning inwards, the defender uses his other hand to trap the attacker's elbow.

4 Oniku daki: continuing to turn towards the attacker with the palms together, the defender has locked the attacker's arm and shoulder with this painful technique.

■ Kuno ichi (female ninja) 1: the female defender is grabbed by the jacket.

2 She steps forward, striking down on the opponent's arm, forcing him towards the floor.

3 She continues the counter-attack with a stamp to the lower leg.

4 Finally, she floors her opponent by locking out his leg with knee pressure.

忍術

a shallow pool of water without making a splash or ripple. In some schools the method is still practised today, although wet rice paper is used instead of water. The paper is laid on the ground and the ninja trainees are required to walk on it without the soles of their feet sticking to it or their feet picking any of it up.

Much of today's practice in the arts of the ninja is done outdoors and students are trained in survival skills and camouflage techniques, as well as basic martial arts and unarmed combat. Also incorporated into the training are night-time combat techniques. Students are taken in groups to various outdoor locations, such as woods or mountains, and taught how to find their way back to the base camp, without the aid of maps or daylight, by navigating by the stars. Outdoors, the ninja instructor will organize his students into two groups. One group heads out into the woods, and after a certain amount of time has elapsed, the second group sets out in search of

■ Claw strike 1: as the defender is gripped by the shoulders, she distracts the attacker with her right hand.

2 She can then unleash a hand claw strike to her attacker's face with the left hand, driving him back.

■ Shuto (side of the hand strike) 1: the defender drops the front defensive hand and evades the attacker's strike by shifting his body weight.

2 He strikes to the underside of the attacker's punching arm with his left fist, simultaneously raising his right arm to head height in a cocked position and beginning to move forward.

3 The defender strikes to the head with a right shuto.

忍術

■ Leg block 1: the attacker grabs the defender's wrist. She strikes her assailant's mid-section with her free elbow.

2 She forces the attacker to the floor by exerting pressure with her knee to execute a leg block.

Hanbo defence 1 : as the attacker throws the punch, the defender drops down, striking to the ribs with the half-length stick.

2 The defender grips the attacker's wrist and steps forward, using the stick as a lever.

3 He steps behind the attacker's leg and forces him down, using the stick as an extension of the arm.

4 Once the attacker is on the floor, he is immobilized by the defender who leans his weight on the stick to trap the arm.

■ Side hand strike and throw 1: the defender steps back, dropping his weight down, while striking the inside of the attacker's punching arm.

2 As he moves forward, the defender grips the attacker's wrist and raises his free arm ready to strike.

them. This friendly game has a serious purpose. The instructor keeps a watchful eye on the way that the students behave, judging their reactions to situations and their ability to cope under stress, and assessing how well they have learned their techniques. The students that are being hunted are expected to use camouflage, to blend in thoroughly with the terrain that surrounds them. The ninja's ability to disappear into his natural surroundings, and his ingenious use of prevailing weather conditions and other natural phenomena, probably give rise to the ancient legend that the ninja could become invisible at will.

Because ninjutsu is called a complete art, students are expected to cope with any combat situation at any moment. The man who is trained only to punch will encounter great difficulty in situations where his punching skills are ineffective. True proficiency in self-protection comes from a blending of all body skills; concentrating on special skills is limiting and dangerous. Hence the emphasis in ninjutsu on outdoor training. Ninja training embraces all the seasons and it is not unusual to find ninja groups training in snow and ice.

Female participation in the art of ninjutsu is smaller than in many other martial arts, although historically the female ninja, who is called a 'kunoichi', played an important role in its early development. Because ninjutsu ex-

tends beyond the normal confines of most martial arts, and in effect becomes a total concept for living, most Western women find that the commitment required by it is too demanding. Kunoichi are trained, just like their male colleagues, in every aspect of the ninja's warrior ways. Traditionally the work of the kunoichi was to gather intelligence, as it was easy for her to enter a household in the guise of a serving maid.

Because the art of ninjutsu differs so much from anything else in the martial arts, it does not have a standard structure of assessment and grading. The length of time required to achieve a dan grade (black belt) is not fixed. Everything depends on the student's understanding and spirit, as well as his expertise in ninja techniques. Only when mind and body accord well will he be awarded any kind of coloured belt of proficiency.

The art of ninjutsu focuses completely on winning, on surviving, coming out on top, at any cost. A thorough training in this unique art equips a student to accomplish this, both in the training hall and in life. Ninjutsu makes no distinction between the two and it is this that puts the ninja one step ahead of other martial artists.

Beyond prowess in physical combat, ninjutsu's incorporation of imagination, personal discipline, perspective, and creative thinking, give the ninja the tools to make him almost undefeatable.

3 He continues to move forward and executes a side hand strike to the neck.

4 Without pausing, the defender steps behind the attacker, forcing him backwards.

5 The defender follows through to throw the attacker backwards over the defender's leg and hip.

■ **ACUPUNCTURE** Chinese system of medicine and healing by the manipulation of needles on certain key points of the body, known as meridians.

■ **AIKIDO** Japanese martial art invented by Morehei Ueshiba, involving internal and external harmony with nature. The techniques of this system are circular in movement. Other styles exist as off-shoots from the original founder's version.

■ **ARNIS DE MANO** Philippine martial art, meaning 'harness of the hand' and involving the use of twin sticks for fighting. It is also a dance in which the fighting art is hidden, devised after the Spanish banned the martial arts.

■ **ATEMI** Japanese art of attacking the vital points of the body. It is much used in jiu jitsu, but is illegal in judo contests.

■ **BALISONG** Correct term for the Filipino butterfly knife, taking its name from the Balisong barrio, in the Philippines, where it was first manufactured. It is a switchblade knife that is opened by a downward wrist action and is much favoured by escrima and kali fighters.

■ **BANDESH** Indian empty-hand fighting technique used to defeat an armed assailant without killing him.

■ **BANDO** Burmese martial art involving numerous boxing methods. It is based upon twelve animals, which are the boar, bull, cobra, deer, eagle, monkey, bird, panther, python, scorpion, tiger and viper. It was introduced into the West by Dr Maung Gyi in 1962.

■ **BANSHAY** Burmese forms of weapon arts, utilizing the staff, sword and spear.

■ **BERSILAT** Martial art of Malaysia, derived from the Indonesian pentjak-silat. It is also practised in Java and Sumatra.

■ **BINOT** Ancient form of weaponless fighting found in India. This art is reputed to be more than 3,000 years old. The word means 'something to protect'. Few practitioners are found today.

■ **BLACK BELT** Belt representing the first significant rank in martial arts training. Achieving this level of proficiency allows one to teach the art to others. In the Japanese ranking system it is known as 'shodan'.

■ **BO** Six-and-a-half-foot staff used by Okinawans and Japanese for combat purposes.

■ **BODHIDHARMA** Indian holy man, also known as Ta'mo and Daruma, credited with bringing Zen Buddhism to China by introducing a series of exercises to the Shaolin temple, traditionally recognized as the origin of all Shaolin kung fu.

■ **BOK HOK PAI** Chinese system of kung fu based upon the mannerisms of the white crane.

■ **BOKKEN** Solid wooden sword used for training purposes in kendo and other martial arts. In the hands of an expert it can deliver fatal blows.

■ **BOK MEI PAI** 'White eyebrow' style of kung fu, named after its founder, Bok Mei. It is a very fast style of kung fu, which legend states to have been banned at the Shaolin temple after Bok Mei killed a fellow student in a fight.

■ **BUSHI** Japanese word meaning 'martial man' to indicate a warrior who follows the code of Bushido ('way of the warrior'). Bushido was a code of ethics, followed by the samurai, which stressed honour, loyalty, duty and obedience. The term has been erroneously used to refer to ancient samurai ways, but it was first coined by the Japanese writer, Inazo Nitobe, in 1892, as the title of his book of the same name.

■ **BUTTERFLY KNIFE** Short, heavy Chinese knife, used in pairs. Its proper name is 'bak jam dao'. It is popularly seen in the kung fu styles of wing chun and hung gar, but other styles have adopted it.

■ **CAT STANCE** Stance used mainly in some karate styles, but also seen in kung fu. It places virtually all the body weight on the back leg. The name derives from its resemblance to a cat about to pounce or spring.

■ **CENTRE LINE** Basic theory of wing chun kung fu, in which students are taught to defend and attack an imaginary line running down through the centre of the body on which all the vital organs are located.

■ **CH'AN (CHAN)** Chinese reading of 'Zen', meaning 'meditation'. In India it is known as 'dhyana'.

■ **CHANG-HON YU** School of taekwondo created by Choi Hong Hi. The name means 'blue cottage'.

■ **CHANG SAN-FENG** Legendary martial arts master and great Taoist philosopher, credited with founding tai chi chuan, one of the three internal systems of Chinese boxing.

■ **CHI** Internal energy, the universal force which is harnessed through a series of special breathing exercises called 'chi-kung' or 'gung'. It brings its users good health and physical strength. Its development is a prime requirement for practitioners of tai chi and hsing-I.

■ **CH'IN-NA** Chinese art of seizing and grappling, identified as a type of wrestling but much more sophisticated. Great knowledge of anatomy is required by its practitioners before the techniques can be successfully applied.

■ **CHIEN (CHEN)** Oldest known style of tai chi chuan. It began in Chien village and has 108 postures.

■ **CHI SAO** Special exercise in wing chun kung fu for developing coordination and sensitivity in the arms. It is also very important for teaching correct elbow-positioning and economy of motion. It is known in the West as 'sticking hands'.

■ **CHOY LI FUT** Southern style of Chinese boxing based upon the Shaolin temple system. It was devised in 1836 by Chan Heung.

■ **CHUAN-FA** Chinese term meaning 'way of the fist', the correct term for kung fu.

■ **CHUDAN** In Japanese martial arts the middle area or chest. In karate this is one of the three target areas of the body.

■ **CHUNGDAN** Korean term to indicate the mid-section of the body, corresponding to the Japanese 'chudan'.

■ **CHUNIN** One of the three ranks in ninjutsu, the middleman.

■ **CRANE** One of the five animal styles of Shaolin kung fu.

■ **DAISENSEI** Title of respect, meaning 'great teacher', given only to a teacher of very high rank.

■ **DAISHO** Matching set of the Japanese long and short swords, worn by all samurai in the Tokugawa era.

■ **DAITO** Japanese long sword with a cutting edge, measuring more than 25 inches. It was used by the samurai.

■ **DAITO-RYU** Style of aiki jutsu from which it is said that aikido developed.

■ **DAN** Japanese term for anyone who has achieved the rank of black belt or above. This term is not exclusive to the martial arts, but is used in many other sports and games, such as swimming and the board game, 'Go'.

■ **DIM MAK** Fabled death touch, a delayed-action strike aimed at an acupuncture meridian, able to cause death to a victim within hours or days of its delivery.

■ **DIT DA JOW** Special herbal ointment, the recipe of which is kept very secret, used to help prevent injury and severe bruising in almost all the Chinese martial arts.

■ **DO** Japanese word for 'path' or 'way', used at the end of the name of a martial art, as in 'karate-do' or 'kendo'.

■ **DOJO** Training place or hall, used for the practice of Japanese martial arts.

■ **DOSHIN-SO** The founder of shorinji kempo, a martial art that is greatly influenced by Chinese systems and is registered in Japan as a religious sect.

■ **DRAGON** One of the five animal styles practised at Shaolin. The mythical dragon symbolizes the spirit and teaches agility and flexibility.

■ **DRUNKEN MONKEY** Style of kung fu based upon the antics of monkeys. Practitioners stagger around as though intoxicated to fool their opponents. The style employs many ground and low techniques.

■ **ELBOW** Close-quarter weapon used in almost all martial systems. It is of particular interest to the muay thai fighters of Thailand.

■ **EMPTY HAND** Literal meaning of karate in Japanese.

■ **ESCRIMA (ESKRIMA)** Martial system of the Philippines that employs sticks, swords and daggers. The term is Spanish and means 'skirmish'. Its adepts are called 'escrimadors'.

■ **FIVE ANCESTORS** Five survivors who escaped during the sacking of the Shaolin temple, credited with being the founders of the Triad societies.

■ **FIVE ANIMALS** Five animals — the crane, dragon, leopard, tiger and snake — whose movements were imitated in a system of fighting said to be the origin of the Shaolin systems.

■ **FORM** Series of choreographed movements in kung fu linking together various martial arts techniques, able to be performed as a solo exercise to aid the practitioner in perfecting his technique. The equivalent in karate is called a 'kata'.

■ **FU HSING** Chinese god of happiness.

■ **FU JOW PAI** 'Tiger claw' system of kung fu, developed at the Shaolin temple.

■ **FULL CONTACT** Form of karate in which full-power kicks are delivered at an opponent. Participants wear protective hand and foot equipment. The sport has grown rapidly in Western countries in the last 10 years.

■ **GEDAN** Lower area of the body, from the waist downwards, in Japanese martial arts.

■ **GENIN** Lowest of three ranks in the ninja hierarchy. A genin was the actual field agent, or ninja, who performed assassinations.

■ **GI** Term used for the training uniform in Japanese martial arts. It is known as a karate-gi in karate and a judo-gi in judo.

■ **GICHIN FUNAKOSHI** Founder of the shotokan style of karate, an Okinawan schoolmaster credited with introducing karate into Japan in 1922.

■ **GOJU-KAI** Offshoot of goju-ryu karate, founded by a student of Miyagi named Gogen Yamaguchi.

■ **GOJU-RYU** One of the major styles of karate developed from Okinawan naha-te. It is a hard-soft system invented by Chojun Miyagi.

■ **GULAT** Type of wrestling found in Java, greatly influenced by sumo wrestling.

■ **GUNG FU** Cantonese pronunciation of kung fu.

■ **GURU** Term of Muslim or Indian origin, applied in many systems of martial arts to a teacher.

■ **GYOJI** Referee at a sumo wrestling match.

■ **HACHIDAN** An 8th-degree black belt ('hachi' means 'eight'). In Japanese martial arts the title denotes a professor of the art.

■ **HADAN** Taekwondo term for the area of the body below the waist, equivalent to the Japanese 'gedan'.

■ **HAKAMA** Long divided skirt-like garment covering the legs and feet, used in kendo, aikido and other Japanese martial arts. The long robe is said to mask the intricate footwork of the practitioner, therefore making it difficult for an opponent to judge his movements.

■ **HAPKIDO** Korean martial art involving many difficult kicks, but also utilizing locks and holds. It is somewhat similar to the Japanese aikido.

■ **HARA-KIRI** Japanese ritual suicide by disembowelment, known in Japan by its proper name of 'seppuku'. It was the ultimate act of atonement by which a samurai warrior regained lost honour.

■ **HARIMAU** 'Tiger' style of pentjak-silat in Indonesia.

■ **HEIAN** Name given to the five basic katas in karate. In some schools the heian katas are also known as pinan katas.

■ **HOJO-JUTSU** Japanese art of binding or rope-tying. First practised by samurai on the battlefield to detain prisoners for questioning. Adepts learn intricate methods of tying up a person with cord.

■ **HO-JUTSU** Samurai art of using firearms.

■ **HOMBU** Headquarters of any martial art.

■ **HOP GAR** Style of kung fu which became prominent during the Ching dynasty of China. It was famous as the official martial art of the Manchu emperors. Two distinct styles within the system were 'white crane' and 'law-horn'. The style is also known by the name 'lama kung fu'.

■ **HORSE STANCE** Basic stance, resembling that of a horse-rider, in many oriental martial arts, especially Chinese hung gar and Japanese karate, in the latter being known as 'kiba dachi'.

■ **HSING-I** Chinese martial art created by the great warrior, Yueh Fei. It is sometimes referred to as 'mind form boxing'. The system is based upon the five Chinese elements.

■ **HUANG TI** Legendary 'Yellow Emperor' of the Chou dynasty, credited as the author of the 'Nei- Ching', the Taoist classic on internal medicine.

■ **HUNG GAR** Style of kung fu stressing powerful hand techniques delivered from low stances. It is based on the movements of the tiger and the crane and is one of the original five ancestor styles. Hung is the creator's name and 'gar' means 'family' or 'system'.

■ **HWARANG DO** 'Way of the flowering manhood', a code of ethics and a fighting system followed by the samurai. The code was also followed in the Silla kingdom of Korea. Today its main advocate in the West is the grandmaster, Joo Bang Lee, who lives in the United States.

■ **HYUNG** Pattern of movements in taekwondo, similar to a form in kung fu and a kata in karate.

■ **IAI-DO** Japanese method of drawing a sword and re-sheathing it, a non-combat art aimed at leading the practitioner to intellectual and spiritual awareness.

■ **IAI-JITSU** Martial system from which iaido was taken, a battlefield art which requires the practitioner to draw his sword rapidly and strike to kill, and then replace it in its scabbard.

■ *I-CHING (Book Of Changes)*, an ancient book of Taoist divination principles. This book, reputed to be the oldest known book in the world, contains the philosophical basis of tai chi chuan, pa-kua, and hsing-I. It comprises 64 six-line symbols, or hexagrams, each composed of two three-line symbols, called trigrams. Together these symbols represent everything that exists in the universe.

■ **IGA** Remote region of Japan famous as the home of the ninja people.

■ **INTERNAL SYSTEMS** There are three internal styles of kung fu: tai chi, pa-kua and hsing-i. They each cultivate *chi* energy, an inherent power within all human beings, largely inexplicable to modern science, which can be unleashed to awesome effect.

■ **IPPON** Full point awarded in martial arts competitions for the flawless execution of a technique.

■ **IRON PALM** Lethal technique of kung fu, able to kill with a single blow. The entire forearm must be conditioned over a period of several years before a practitioner is able to attain any reasonable standard. This conditioning makes the adept's hand and arm like an iron bar.

■ **JKA** Japan Karate Association, founded in 1955. It is the largest karate association in the world. Its first chief instructor was the founder of shotokan, Gichin Funakoshi.

■ **JEET KUNE DO** Style of kung fu devised by the late Bruce Lee. Its name means 'way of the intercepting fist'.

■ **JIU JITSU** Japanese martial art based upon the exploitation of an opponent's strength against himself. The name means 'soft' or 'flexible' and the art contains both armed and unarmed techniques.

■ **JODAN** In Japanese martial arts the top area of the body, from the shoulders upward.

■ **JONIN** Highest rank in the ninja hierarchy. A jonin received instructions directly from a lord.

■ **JUDO** Modern sporting form of jiu jitsu, developed by Dr Jigoro Kano in 1882 and to date the only oriental martial art included in the Olympic games.

■ **JUDOKA** One who practises judo.

■ **JUKEN-DO** 'Way of the bayonet', a Japanese martial art that has recently adopted a sporting format. It consists of fighting with a bayonet fixed to the end of a rifle and developed primarily from spear and staff arts.

■ **JUTSU (JITSU)** Japanese word meaning 'skill' or 'art'.

■ **JUTTE (JITTE)** Single-tined or pronged iron truncheon, used by the early Japanese police force. The single tine at the hilt of the weapon enables the user to trap a katana (sword) without being injured by the blade.

■ **KALARIPAYIT** Indian system of martial training, of which two styles exist, the northern and the southern. It is chiefly practised by the Tamils in the south and decendants of the Nayar warriors in the north. The word means 'battlefield training'.

■ **KALI** Martial art practised in the Philippines, consisting of 12 categories or disciplines. Beginners learn to use weapons first and empty-hand methods last. Its adepts claim that it is a complete martial system.

■ **KAMA** Ancient Asian agricultural implement, similar to the sickle. It was developed as a weapon on the island of Okinawa. Today a wooden version is used as a training device in karate and other Japanese martial arts.

■ **KARATE (KARATE-DO)** 'Way of the empty hand', a Japanese martial art employing kicks and strikes delivered to all areas of the body. It was developed largely on Okinawa and owes much to Chinese systems of combat.

■ **KARATEKA** One who practises karate.

■ **KATA** Series of set movements in karate, in which the martial artist defends himself against imaginary opponents. It is considered by many of the founding masters of karate to be the 'soul of the art'.

■ **KATANA** Japanese sword.

■ **KEMPO** Japanese pronunciation of 'ch'uan fa', the Chinese for 'way of the fist'. It is a form of karate based upon Chinese systems and Korean taekwondo which uses high-speed blocks and counter-attacks and also spectacular kicking techniques. It is very popular in the United States.

■ **KENDO** Modern Japanese fencing based upon the ancient warrior skill of kenjutsu. In the sporting form the live blade is replaced by a bamboo equivalent called a 'shinai'.

■ **KI** Japanese translation of the Chinese 'chi', the vital, intrinsic energy within the human body. The development of ki is strived for in such martial arts as aikido and hapkido.

■ **KIAI** Super-shout or yell in Japanese martial arts, emitted when applying a technique to add extra power and stun an opponent.

■ **KIHON** Basic training moves, repeated many times in order to reach proficiency.

■ **KOBUDO** Name referring to the ancient martial ways of the Japanese warrior.

■ **KRABI-KRABBONG** Twin-sworded combat system of Thailand, in which practitioners fight at lightning speeds using two razor-sharp short swords or a sword and a shield.

■ **KUNG FU** A derivative of a Chinese term meaning 'hard work and applied skills'; now accepted by both Westerners and orientals as a generic term for martial art skills.

■ **KUP** In taekwondo one of the eight grades of ranking before the black belt, comparable to the Japanese 'kyu' grade.

■ **KUSARIGAMA** Sickle attached by a long chain to a weighted end, a trapping and ensnaring weapon highly popular among the ninja people.

■ **KYOKUSHINKAI** Japanese karate system founded by the Korean-born Masatatsu Oyama. Its name means 'way of ultimate truth'. Oyama gained fame by fighting bulls barehanded. He still holds the world record for breaking the largest number of roofing tiles with one blow.

■ **KYUDO** 'Way of the bow', a Japanese martial art of archery which incorporates deep Zen concepts. Great emphasis is placed upon the way in which one applies oneself during the ritual of preparing the arrow for flight. Actually hitting the target is of little importance.

■ **LAO TSU** Legendary sage in Chinese history, credited with founding the principles of Taoism.

■ **LATHI (LATHE)** Indian art of fighting with a staff.

■ **LO HAN** Name of any famous disciple of Buddha and also the name of the exercises that Bodhidharma taught to the monks at Shaolin when he found them in an emaciated condition. The method of training known as 'the 18 hands of the lo han' is the basis of what we now know as kung fu.

■ **LUNG** Chinese word meaning 'dragon'.

■ **MABUNI KENWA** Creator of shitoryu karate, who studied under the same Okinawan master, called Hosu, as Funakoshi.

■ **MAKIWARA** Striking post used to condition the hands and feet in karate.

■ **MARTIAL ARTS** Term denoting the arts of war, taken from 'Mars', the god of war. It now means a fighting discipline to promote combat proficiency.

■ **MEN** Face mask or helmet used in kendo.

■ **MOO DUK KWAN** Korean term for an academy for martial practice.

■ **MOOK JOONG** Wooden dummy, shaped like a man, used for conditioning and training purposes in many hard, or external, styles of kung fu, notably wing chun and hung gar.

■ **MUAY THAI** Correct term for Thai boxing.

■ **NAGINATA** Japanese halberd, or curved-bladed spear, used in the martial way of Naginata-do. This art was adopted by women and is now a thriving combat sport in Japan, although the spear tip has been replaced with a piece of bamboo for safety reasons.

■ **NAHA TE** One of the three original styles of Okinawan karate, named after the town of Naha, where it was first practised.

■ **NINJA** Secret society of highly-trained assassins in old Japan, trained from birth to become expert in a vast number of martial skills. It is also the term for a male exponent of ninjutsu.

■ **NINJUTSU** Martial art of the ninja people. The original name was 'shinobi'.

■ **NUNCHAKU** Two wooden batons linked by a short chain or cord to make an awesome weapon. Used originally as a rice flail, it is found in most cultures throughout Asia.

■ **OKINAWA TE** Collective term for the schools of Okinawan karate. The name means 'Okinawa hand'.

■ **PA-KUA** Style of kung fu, based on circular movements with open-palm strikes. It means 'eight trigrams' and the concept comes from the classic Chinese treatise, the *I-Ching*, or *Book of Changes*. The practitioner constantly changes directions during an attack. Hence the art is sometimes known as 'eight- directions palm boxing'.

■ **PENTJAK-SILAT** Indonesian martial art of Muslim and Chinese origin. Many hundreds of styles exist.

■ **PRAYING MANTIS** Style of kung fu known in China as 'tong long'. It is named after Wong Long, who invented the style after witnessing a fight between a grasshopper and a praying mantis.

■ **RANDORI** In judo, free practice or sparring in which the techniques are not prescribed.

■ **ROKUSHAKUBO** Okinawan six-foot staff or pole made from oak or similar hardwood. 'Roku' means 'six', 'shaku' means 'about a foot in length', and 'bo' means 'pole' or 'staff'.

■ **ROUNDHOUSE KICK** Kick used in virtually all the martial arts. Its circular path gives it extra power by generating a centrifugal force and it is one of the most powerful kicks in the martial artist's arsenal.

■ **RYU** 'School' or 'style' in Japanese martial arts.

■ **SAI** Three-pronged, fork-like weapon, once made of iron, now of steel. It resembles a short, blunt sword and is a single-handed weapon used in pairs.

■ **SAMURAI** Japanese feudal warrior. The word means 'one who serves'. A samurai served as a military retainer to a lord and his shogun. A masterless samurai was known as a 'ronin'.

■ **SANCHIN** Breathing exercise of 20 movements used in Okinawan karate. It teaches a practitioner to tense his body and control his breathing during intense combat.

■ **SAVATE** French system of foot fighting, correctly termed 'la savate'. It was the forerunner of traditional French boxing, called 'la boxe française', used in Paris by the underworld. It was influenced by Chinese martial arts.

■ **SENSEI** Japanese word for a teacher or instructor.

■ **SHAOLIN** Temple in the Songshan Mountains of northern China, where kung fu is said to have been born.

■ **SHIAI** Contest in kendo in which two kendoka use a variety of techniques to score points.

■ **SHINAI** Bamboo sword made of four strips bound together, used in kendo to replace the live blade.

■ **SHINOBI** Old term from which the name 'ninja' derives.

■ **SHINTO** Japanese animistic religion, meaning 'way of the gods'. It is based on ancestor worship.

■ **SHORINJI KEMPO** Japanese karate system founded by Doshin So, now deceased. Its organization is now headed by his daughter.

■ **SHOTOKAN** School of Japanese karate founded by Gichin Funakoshi. The name derives from Funakoshi's pen name of 'Shoto'. It is probably the most widely practised style of karate in the world.

■ **SHUAI CHIAO** One of the earliest organized fighting systems in China, dating from c.700 BC. It was a form of wrestling, but with few throws. Today it is an official sport of the People's Republic of China.

■ **SHURIKEN** Sharp-pointed throwing stars, originally made of iron, a favourite weapon of the ninja. Many shapes and sizes existed.

■ **SIFU** Instructor in kung fu, corresponding to a 'sensei' in karate. The word means 'father'.

■ **SIKARAN** Martial art found on the Philippine island of Luzon. It stresses kicks and leg techniques and resembles some Japanese martial arts.

■ **SIL LIM TAO** Primary form in wing chun, meaning 'little idea' or 'little imagination'. The form teaches elbow-positioning and the protection of the centre line. It has no foot movements.

■ **SIL LUM** Cantonese name for the Shaolin temple.

■ **SO-JUTSU** Japanese skill in using the spear. The name means 'art of the spear'.

■ **SPARRING** Combat experience to give a karate student the opportunity to apply the techniques he has learned.

■ **SPORT KARATE** Karate competition in which contestants fight under combat rules in a ring or area. They wear protective gloves and foot pads. Techniques are scored and points are given. Actual combat is prohibited, although some leeway is allowed.

■ **SUMO** Ancient form of Japanese wrestling, steeped in quasi-religious aspects of Shintoism. Contestants build themselves up to great weights in order to gain an advantage over their opponents.

■ **SUN TZU (SUN TSU)** Author of the Chinese military classic, *The Art Of War*, believed by many to be the treatise upon which ninjutsu is based.

■ **SWEEP** Technique which catches the opponent's foot or feet and unbalances him.

■ **TAEKWONDO** Korean style of empty-hand combat very similar to karate. Great emphasis is placed upon delivering strikes with the feet and fists. This art was partly indigenous to Korea, being known as tae kyon in its older version.

■ **TAI CHI CHUAN (TAI CHAI)** One of the three internal systems of kung fu. Much value is placed upon its therapeutic properties for the relief of stress and tension. It is intended to guide one into a state of peace and tranquility. The word means 'great ultimate fist'. There is a deadly side to this art, but it is known by only a few instructors.

■ **TAMASHIWARA** Japanese technique of using strikes with the body against materials such as wood, tiles, bricks and ice to test the power of a strike.

■ **TANG SOO DO** 'Way of the tang hand', a Korean martial arts system very similar to Japanese shotokan karate. The style was developed in 1949 by Hwang Kee, who claimed to have derived it from the ancient Korean arts of t'ang su and subak.

■ **TAO** Chinese term meaning 'path' or 'way'. Tao is an invisible force or energy, present in all things in the universe.

■ **TE** Okinawan term meaning 'hand'.

■ **THAI BOXING** See **MUAY THAI**.

■ **THAING** General term for the Burmese arts of self-defence.

■ **TIGER** One of the five animals in Shaolin kung fu.

■ **TOBOK** Suit or tunic worn by practitioners of taekwondo, consisting of a loose shirt and trousers tied in the middle with a sash or belt.

■ **TONFA** Okinawan agricultural implement, the handle used to operate a manual millstone, adopted by the Okinawans as a weapon to fight the invading Japanese with. It is used in karate to improve technique. In recent times many United States police departments have issued an updated version of the tonfa to their officers as a replacement for the billy club or night stick.

■ **UESHIBA** Morihei Ueshiba, the founder of Aikido.

■ **URUMI** Indian spring-sword with four sharp edges.

■ **VITAL POINTS** Certain areas on the body which, when struck in a particular way, cause great pain or death.

■ **WADO RYU KARATE** 'Way of peace', style of Japanese karate developed from shotokan by Hironori Ohtsuka.

■ **WAZARI** In competitive martial arts a score of half a point, awarded for the skilful execution of a technique.

■ **WHITE BELT** Colour of belt to indicate a beginner in most Japanese martial arts.

■ **WING CHUN** Chinese martial art invented by a woman named Yim Wing Chun. Its name means 'beautiful springtime'. It is considered by many to be one of the most effective forms of kung fu in existence. The fundamental premise of the style is economy of motion. Wing chun greatly influenced Bruce Lee when he was formulating his own eclectic system of jeet kune do.

■ **WU SHU** Chinese term for the military arts, now used as a generic name for the highly acrobatic martial arts of mainland China.

■ **YANG** In Chinese cosmology the positive aspect of the universe, relating to hardness, masculinity and light, one half of the Taoist view of the universe.

■ **YANG STYLE** Style of tai chi, developed by Yang Lu Chan in the early part of the 19th century. It contains the original 13 tai chi postures.

■ **YIN** In Chinese cosmology, the negative aspect of the universe, relating to emptiness, softness, darkness and femininity. Yin is represented as a black fish with a white eye in the famous yin-yang symbol.

■ **YOKO ARUKI** Ninja secret walking techniques. The word means 'walking sideways'. By employing such methods the ninja did not reveal in which direction he was travelling, thus making it difficult for his enemies to track him.

■ **YOKOZUNA** Grand champion rank of sumo wrestling, the highest of five ranks.

■ **YUDANSHA** Kendoka who has achieved the rank of black belt or higher, alone permitted to wear an outfit of a uniform colour.

■ **ZANSHIN** State of mind cultivated in many Japanese martial arts. The practitioner is supposed to become calm yet fully aware of his opponent's every movement.

■ **ZEN** Religious philosophy that claims that one can reach satori, or enlightenment, through meditation. Founded by the Indian monk and holy man Bodhidharma. Zen makes use of paradoxical poems called koans to clear the mind of trivia and so reach the meditative state required. In China Zen is called chan or ch'an. Zen was much favoured by the Japanese samurai.

■ **ZHURKANE** Persian (Iranian) term meaning 'powerhouse'. It refers to a system of highly specialized strength exercises and professes to be a martial art dating back more than 3,000 years to the court of Darius.

LEARNING RESOURCE CENTRE
TH⬚⬚⬚⬚⬚⬚⬚⬚ ⬚ERHAM COLLEGE
M⬚⬚⬚⬚⬚⬚ ROAD
R⬚⬚⬚⬚⬚AM
S60 2⬚⬚⬚
TEL: 01709 300696